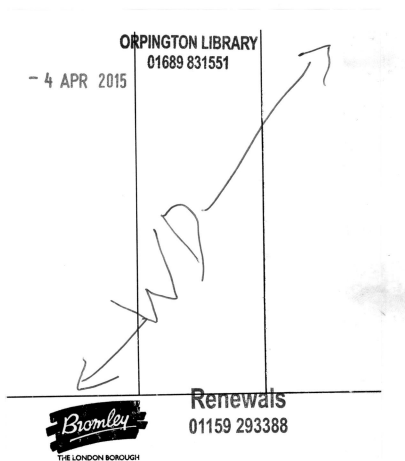

FAMILY HISTORY FROM PEN & SWORD

TRACING YOUR ANCESTORS' PARISH RECORDS

A Guide for Family and Local Historians

Stuart A. Raymond

Pen & Sword
FAMILY HISTORY

First published in Great Britain in 2014
PEN & SWORD FAMILY HISTORY
an imprint of
Pen & Sword Books Ltd
47 Church Street
Barnsley
South Yorkshire
S70 2AS

ISBN 978 1 78303 044 6

A CIP catalogue record for this book is
available from the British Library.

Typeset in Palatino and Optima by
CHIC GRAPHICS

Printed and bound in England by
CPI Group (UK), Croydon, CR0 4YY

Pen & Sword Books Ltd incorporates the imprints of Pen & Sword
Archaeology, Atlas, Aviation, Battleground, Discovery, Family History, History,
Maritime, Military, Naval, Politics, Railways, Select, Social History, Transport,
True Crime, and Claymore Press, Frontline Books, Leo Cooper, Praetorian
Press, Remember When, Seaforth Publishing and Wharncliffe.

For a complete list of Pen & Sword titles please contact
PEN & SWORD BOOKS LTD
47 Church Street, Barnsley, South Yorkshire, S70 2AS, England
E-mail: enquiries@pen-and-sword.co.uk
Website: www.pen-and-sword.co.uk

CONTENTS

ACKNOWLEDGEMENTS
AND PREFACE

This book depends heavily on the publications of countless local historians. Unfortunately there are far too many to mention them all individually but I hope they will accept this collective acknowledgement. My apologies to any who may have been cited without due acknowledgement.

I have also depended heavily on the resources of the various libraries I have used. They are too many to name here but a special thanks goes to librarians in Trowbridge who obtained innumerable interlibrary loans for me. Thanks, too, to those who read my manuscript in draft: Simon Fowler and one of my students who wishes to remain anonymous. Finally, thanks go to my wife Marjorie, who drags me away from the computer whenever I have been there too long.

The original draft of this book contained far too many endnotes and I have had to prune them drastically. References to specific local records have therefore not been noted as it should be easy to identify the locations of the originals (although I have mostly used published sources).

Stuart Raymond
April 2014

Chapter 1

WHAT CAN YOU DO WITH PARISH RECORDS?

If you want to know how life was lived in past centuries, then you will find much useful information in parish records. They are far from being the dull and boring documents that those who have not read them might think. Among the papers from the parish chest are records of the devotion of medieval parishioners to their church, the iconoclasm that wrecked most medieval church art, the church ales [festivals] that offended puritan sensibilities, the violence of being whipped 'at the cart's tail', the tragedies of sudden death, the property that was divided up when the land was enclosed, the accusations of disreputable practices levied against both clergy and laity, the penny-pinching of many vestries, the arguments over the cost of the poor, the kindness shown to young men who benefited from apprenticeships funded by charities, the beliefs that persuaded churchwardens to assist sufferers from the King's Evil [scrofula] seeking a cure from the touch of the monarch, and the wickedness of Poor Laws that forced removal even when young girls were about to be delivered of their illegitimate children. However, perhaps we should not judge eighteenth-century parishioners by twenty-first-century standards.

There are many ways in which these documents can be used. The family historian is particularly well served by registers of baptisms, marriages and burials, vital for the compilation of pedigrees. He or she can also find burials recorded in churchwardens' accounts, which may detail fees paid for ringing the bells, for hiring the bier and for the burial itself. Relationships may be recorded in bastardy orders, settlement examinations and apprenticeship records. Researchers will also find names in a multiplicity of different parish records. They can be used not merely to construct the bare bones of a pedigree but also to place one's family in its historical context. The parochial offices held by family members, the property they owned, the apprenticeships they served, the work that they did, the religion that they practised; all may be revealed by parish records. There are numerous lists of names, helping to place ancestors in time and place and sometimes recording their houses and farms. The names of ratepayers are listed in the

1

accounts of churchwardens and other officers or perhaps in separate rate assessments. Easter books list parishioners and their offerings; pew lists and plans reveal the relative status of everyone in the parish. Landowners and occupiers can be identified in enclosure awards and tithe apportionments, which can be usefully compared with nineteenth-century census returns.

The local historian is also well served by these records. They provide the basis for research in many topics, such as demography, landscape history, religious history and agricultural history. Sometimes they throw useful light on national affairs: for example, the Upton (Nottinghamshire) constables' accounts reveal much interesting information concerning the civil war, as do those of Stathern (Leicestershire). However, their value is much greater than that. Many works of great importance for English history depend upon them. Parish registers, for example, form the basis of Schofield & Wrigley's *The Population History of England 1541–1871* (1981), which provided a new model for understanding the way in which population grew over three centuries. Similarly, churchwardens' accounts written by the sixteenth-century priest of Morebath (Devon) form the basis for Eamon Duffy's *The Voices of Morebath* (Yale University Press, 2003); a groundbreaking study showing how the Reformation was greeted in a remote Devonshire parish. Duffy's work complemented Robert Whiting's *The Blind Devotion of the People: Popular Religion and the English Reformation* (Cambridge University Press, 1989), which described popular reactions to the Reformation in Devon and Cornwall and also drew heavily on churchwardens' accounts.

The reaction of most Englishmen to the Reformation has been characterized as 'stoical compliance with, rather than enthusiasm for, the new protestantism'.[1] The evidence that supports such conclusions is to be found in churchwardens' accounts, which frequently reveal tardy compliance with demands for the destruction of altars and images but quick compliance with the demands of Mary's government for their reinstatement. As long ago as 1853, John Bruce was able to demonstrate from their accounts that the churchwardens of Minchinhampton (Gloucestershire) acted with alacrity when Queen Mary restored the old religion. He also demonstrated their tardiness in abandoning Mass when Protestantism returned in 1558. It was not until 1575, when a new rector was installed, that 6s 8d was spent on 'pullynge down, destroying, and throwing out of the church, sundry superstitious things tending to the maintenance of idolatry'.[2]

Accounts that show heavy expenditure on church towers, new naves and sometimes entirely new churches clearly demonstrate that late-medieval English Catholicism was vibrant until the last breath of Queen Mary. If further evidence is needed, then a walk in the country is likely to provide it:

Broughton Gifford (Wiltshire) church tower.

in most counties it is not possible to go more than 3 or 4 miles without seeing an example of a church renovated or rebuilt in the fifteenth or early sixteenth century. Parish records may well contain evidence for the work undertaken.

Accounts can also be used by economic historians. The Upton accounts mentioned above provide a glimpse of the village as an economic unit during the civil war. Constables knew where to find labourers to work on the bulwarks at Newark, men to conscript as soldiers, or scriveners able to write their warrants and accounts. Their purchases for the army indicate who were the main producers of goods, who could provide transport for goods being sent to Nottingham and who had houses large enough to accommodate soldiers. Bread and ale could be obtained; so could linen. The agricultural historian can see who produced dairy products, where peas could be obtained and who grew wheat, barley and rye. Sheep, pigs and ducks were also available.

Social historians can find a great deal of information in other parish records. K.D.M. Snell's *Annals of the Labouring Poor: Social Change and Agrarian England, 1660–1900* (Cambridge University Press, 1985) uses settlement examinations extensively to construct a picture of the 'labouring poor'. Patterns of seasonal unemployment, the decline of traditional apprenticeship and family formation are among the topics investigated. Poor Law records provide valuable evidence on the terms of employment of agricultural labourers and can be used to trace their migrations. In Berkshire, they provide useful evidence for hiring fairs.[3] Settlement certificates record the migration of the poor. So do the accounts of overseers and constables: the Upton constables' accounts, for example, record that at least fifty-eight Irish migrants (and many others) received relief in this Nottinghamshire village in 1646–7, despite the fact that it was not on a main route to anywhere. Paupers' letters can be used to study the attitudes and strategies of the poor themselves.[4]

Enclosure awards, tithe apportionments and associated maps tell us much about both social structure and agricultural history. The maps enable historical geographers to trace the development of the landscape over previous centuries. Tithe maps are one of the few sources that enable crops to be linked to particular fields. Tithe and enclosure records, combined with parish registers and the census, enable us to reconstruct entire historical communities and to repopulate particular houses and hamlets.

Care does, of course, have to be taken in interpreting parish records. If you are writing a parish history, a wider perspective is needed; the history of the parish cannot adequately be written from its parish records alone. The astute investigator will use them in conjunction with documents drawn from other sources such as Quarter Sessions, the diocese, local estate records and The National Archives. Parish records alone are partial and are unlikely to reveal the total history of a particular place.

Researchers should always be aware of the limitations of their documents. Churchwardens' accounts, for example, obviously reflect the fiscal activities of the churchwardens. However, they are far from being complete records of parish history; even on their own terms, they do not necessarily record all the income that churchwardens received or all the expenses they met, and may therefore give a misleading impression of parochial finances. St Andrew Hubbard was not one of the wealthiest parishes in London; however, the Edwardian inventory of its goods reveals that it was much better provided for than might have been expected from an examination of its churchwardens' accounts.[5]

Accounts do not explain the reasons behind churchwardens' activities; those have to be inferred. They have little to say directly about the non-fiscal affairs of the parish; they provide very limited information on the activities of the clergy or on other parish affairs, although they may allow some inferences to be drawn. They should be used in conjunction with other parish records along with other sources.

It is not so obvious that churchwardens' accounts might also have non-fiscal purposes. The accounts of All Saints, Bristol were compiled by its vicar, who 'laboured to compile and make this book for to be a memorial and remembrance for ever, for the curates and churchwardens that shall be'. How did that aim influence the contents of his book? It includes a formal copy of fifteenth-century churchwardens' accounts, evidently written to celebrate the importance of the contribution made by churchwardens to the parish. However, is the copy always accurate? Its editor has demonstrated that there were important omissions and in particular that the substantial contribution to parish life made by one churchwarden who subsequently fell out of favour was ignored.[6] It is therefore vital that the researcher views his sources with a critical eye.

Chapter 2

THE ENGLISH PARISH AND ITS GOVERNMENT

The Parish: Origins & History

The English parish has played a key role in English life for at least a thousand years. Our ancestors lived in a very close-knit society; neighbours were frequently neighbours for life. The parish gave a framework for their lives, both religious and secular, and it offered security. Parishioners met together every Sunday in church. A whole host of services, ranging from charities to policing, from roads to vermin eradication, were provided by the parish. In return, it imposed sometimes onerous demands on parishioners. Their presence in church was compulsory. Householders were expected to contribute to 'collections', to pay rates, to serve in parish office and to help maintain the roads. Paupers might receive relief from

Charlton Musgrove (Somerset) Church.

Great Chalfield Church.

poverty but might also be unable to leave their own parish. Belonging to a parish provided substantial benefits but also imposed serious obligations.

Many parishes have existed for over a millennia; others have been divided, subdivided or expanded over the centuries. The origins of most ancient parishes are lost in the mists of antiquity, although it is clear that they played an important role in the development of the medieval church.

Celtic Christianity was driven out of southern Britain during the Anglo-Saxon invasions but the faith was re-established in England by the sixth-century mission of St Augustine. His missionaries fanned out across the country, erecting wooden crosses where the gospel was preached. Gradually, wood was replaced by stone and, perhaps centuries later, by churches. Minster churches provided bases from which large areas could be served. Landowners built churches beside their houses or castles to serve their own estates. In Week St Mary (Cornwall), the field next to the church is known as Castle Ditches; the De Wyke family had their castle there in the twelfth century. Many churches adjoining manor houses can still be seen. Great Chalfield (Wiltshire) and Dyrham (Gloucestershire) provide classic illustrations of this juxtaposition. The parish was the religious equivalent of the manor.

Landed estates frequently gave their boundaries to parishes. Most of medieval Stourton (Wiltshire) was owned by the Stourton family, who probably built its church. Some parishes were founded by ecclesiastics, or by the minster whose territory was being encroached upon. Jurisdictional

Dyrham Church.

and financial issues had to be settled when new churches were built. Could their priests baptize babies or bury the dead? The right to do so sometimes required payment to mother churches, which may be recorded even in seventeenth-century accounts. When John Leland, the sixteenth-century antiquary, visited Chew Magna (Somerset), he reported that 'there be dyvers paroche chirches there aboute that once a year do homage unto Chute their mother chyrche'. Sometimes a new church became merely a township chapel in a much larger parish. There were, for instance, twenty-four townships in the parish of Malpas (Cheshire). A single parish could have many chapels. In the fourteenth and fifteenth centuries many landowners built private chapels for themselves. These had no direct connection to the parish, although a bishop's licence was required.

The process of establishing a parochial structure was encouraged by the fact that by 930 everyone had to pay tithe – one tenth of one's income – to the church. Originally this was paid to minsters but the right to receive it was gradually transferred to new parish churches. The old minsters gradually ceased to have more than parochial status.

The founders of new churches owned them, appointed the clergy who served them, and retained control over income such as tithe. The advowson – the right to appoint clergy – descended to founders' heirs. Bishops were powerless to check the dismemberment of the minster system, to supervise the new parishes or to ensure that priests were fit for office. Abuses were inevitable, provoking a reaction. The Gregorian reform movement demanded an end to lay ownership of parish churches and insisted on the right of bishops to institute priests to their benefices. The First Lateran Council (1123) decreed that 'the appointment of priests to churches belongs to the bishops, and without their consent they may not receive tithes and churches from laymen'. Patrons could not, however, be deprived of their property rights. Consequently, they continued to choose priests for their churches but first presented them to the bishop, who instituted them to their livings.

The Gregorian demands coincided with the needs of many owners of churches, mostly wealthy knights and barons. They frequently lived violent lives and needed a way of atoning for their sins. Many gave their churches to endow monasteries, where monks would pray for their souls in perpetuity. The monasteries became corporate rectors with the right to tithe, and appointed vicars to serve their cures. Vicars might be paid a stipend or receive a portion of tithe or other income. Monasteries, as rectors, appropriated most revenue for their own purposes, although they were responsible for maintaining chancels. By 1530 over 4,000 advowsons were in monastic hands.

Vicars, however, could not afford to maintain their churches. Consequently, the laity was assigned responsibility for the maintenance of naves and churchyards. The Synod of Exeter in 1287 required parishioners, in addition to paying tithe, to accept responsibility for maintaining naves and churchyards, while rectors retained responsibility for chancels.

Meanwhile, the concept of the parish was further refined. Parishes were expected to be self-sufficient. Their tithes were owned by the rector, who also required an endowment of glebe land. Parishioners were expected to attend church, to have their babies baptized and themselves buried in the churchyard. Fixed geographical boundaries were needed in order to ensure that people knew where to pay their tithes and to attend worship.

The parochial system did not grow in accordance with a pre-ordained plan. Anomalies inevitably developed. There were many peculiars; that is, parishes outside of the jurisdiction of the diocesan bishop. Uffculme (Devon), for example, was under the jurisdiction of the Dean of Salisbury.

Westminster Abbey was a royal peculiar, under the direct authority of the Crown. Many parishes had detached portions. The parish of Holme Cultram (Cumberland) had four townships, containing no less than 101 detached portions. Some places, such as the Scilly Isles (Cornwall), were extra-parochial, being under the authority of no parish.

Until the twelfth century, boundaries had not necessarily been set; henceforth, they became cast in stone and it was rare for them to be altered until the nineteenth century. The importance of remembering them was emphasized by the beating of the bounds at Rogationtide. In 1691 the boys of Week St Mary (Cornwall) were whipped as they perambulated the bounds, in order to help their memory. They were given figs in recompense!

Parish boundaries were important for a variety of reasons: they determined paupers' settlement; they governed liability for parish rates; they determined who had the right to communal resources such as commons. They also engendered a sense of belonging.

The average area of a parish was roughly 3,790 acres. There was, however, considerable variation. Small parishes abounded in the southern counties and in cities. In the north, by contrast, parishes were frequently huge with numerous townships and chapelries. Whalley (Lancashire) comprised no fewer than 103,395 acres.

Many new churches were founded or re-founded in the twelfth and thirteenth centuries. Episcopal registers of the period are full of the records of church dedications. Change in subsequent centuries was limited: only twelve new parishes were created in Devon between 1291 and 1535.[1]

When Edward I collected a tax to go on crusade in 1291, his collectors were able to identify over 8,000 parishes.[2] The *Valor Ecclesiasticus* of 1535 listed 8,838 churches. When John Rickman reported on the results of the 1801 census, he reckoned that there were 11,271 parishes, although that figure included some chapelries. It was not always clear when a chapelry might be considered to hold parochial status. In the Victorian era, numerous new parishes were created in urban areas; more recently, many parishes have been amalgamated in united benefices or team ministries. There are now 12,500 parishes and 16,000 church buildings, with 8,030 full-time equivalent-paid clergy, plus another 3,000 non-stipendiary ministers.[3]

By the fifteenth century, the church and its parish were well-established as the ritual centre of the community. They provided the focus for most Englishmen's sense of community and for a wide variety of activities; secular, religious, private and governmental. While the mass – or, after the Reformation, the sermon – was seen by clerics as its central function, there was much more to church life than that. Birth, marriage and death were all major occasions for the expression of communal feeling. Birth brought babies to the font for baptism. Weddings were celebrated in the church porch. Death meant burial in the churchyard or, for the wealthier, in the church.

The church building was not seen as being set apart solely for its spiritual function until the Victorian era. It was used for a variety of secular functions and served as a meeting place for both sacred and profane purposes. Business was conducted in the porch, church ales were held in the nave, and manorial and ecclesiastical courts, as well as vestry meetings, might be held in the vestry. Parish chests could be used as safe deposit boxes for private papers. Parish armour and fire-fighting equipment were stored in the tower. During times of conflict, the building might be used for defence.

The parish was increasingly used for the purposes of secular government. When the Domesday Book was compiled in 1086, the unit used was the manor. A century later, in 1188, the Saladin tithe, used to finance a crusade, was collected through the parish. Parishes became more viable units of assessment than secular landholdings, since their boundaries ceased to fluctuate. Pre-Reformation churchwardens raised as much money from their parishes as the Crown received in direct lay taxes or lords received in rent.[4]

Under the Tudors and Stuarts, parishes took on a variety of secular functions: poor relief (from 1536), highway maintenance (from 1555), and even the extermination of vermin (from 1533). In succeeding centuries, parish officers exercised considerable power over parishioners. However, after 1662, nonconformity began to offer an alternative focus of loyalty. By the mid-nineteenth century, it attracted around half the churchgoing population. Admittedly, many non-attendees retained a residual loyalty to the Church of England whose priests baptized, married and buried them, but commitment to the church was declining. Industrialization and secularization steadily weakened the link between parish church and parishioner in the late eighteenth and nineteenth centuries. The parish was ceasing to be a community, the church was ceasing to matter in many people's lives, and the secular functions of parish vestries began to be seen as increasingly anomalous.

An Act of 1818 introduced the concept of the ecclesiastical parish without secular responsibilities. These were to be created in parishes which needed to be subdivided and where new churches were to be built. Secular functions were left to the civil parishes, which continued to cover the original areas of subdivided parishes.

The aim of this Act was to build new churches. In practice, it paved the way for the transfer of civil functions to other organizations. Turnpike trusts had already removed main highways from parish responsibility, and

Improvement Commissioners had taken over a variety of functions in towns. Responsibility for the poor was transferred to Poor Law Unions in 1834; responsibility for policing was lost in 1856; church rates were abolished in 1864; responsibility for roads was transferred to local Highway Boards in 1865; municipal and private cemeteries increasingly took responsibility for burying the dead; separate parish councils took responsibility for any remaining secular functions in 1894.

Power and authority were important aspects of communal identity and were reflected in the responsibilities laid on parish officers, but voluntarism and the willingness of the laity to participate in parish life were also vital. In many medieval parishes, guilds provided a major outlet for lay initiative.

Guilds

Medieval guilds sustained and encouraged religious observance. They existed in order to pray for the souls of both present and former members, to assist sick or impoverished members and to support widows and orphans. They usually had wardens and sometimes employed chaplains. Funds were raised by subscription or by social events such as ales. Sometimes they received substantial bequests.

Guilds were frequently run by specific social groups. At Croscombe (Somerset) there were guilds for the 'Younglings', the 'Maidens', the Webbers (weavers), the Tuckers (fullers), the Archers and the Hogglers (labourers). In fifteenth-century Bodmin (Cornwall) there were forty such brotherhoods. Five were craft guilds but the rest were devoted primarily to religious observances under the patronage of particular saints.

Guilds played an important role in the process of forging community identities. Some of their activities can be followed in churchwardens' accounts and other parish records. These are basic sources for parish history and will be examined in Chapter 3. They were created by clergy and parish officers, whose role must now be considered.

The Clergy

The evolution of the parish was accompanied by an evolution of what it meant to be a cleric. Before the Reformation, the church emphasized priestly separateness, especially by demanding celibacy, but required very little education from ordinands. Most were drawn from humble origins. The priest had to be able to say the mass; that was all. Few attended university; few could preach. Consequently, when the Reformation came, there were too few preachers to spread the gospel. The reformed ministry, with its emphasis on preaching, required much higher educational standards than those held by most priests in the mid-sixteenth century. Clergy ceased to be celibate, and introduced a new figure into parish life: the clergyman's wife. However, many old figures disappeared: there were, for example, no chantry clergy. At this point, clergy numbers slumped.

Yet the social distance between incumbents and their parishioners grew. The clergyman's wife was not the only new figure in the post-Reformation church. The gentleman in holy orders also appeared. He could afford to pay for the university education required by the reformers. The church gradually became a serious option for the younger sons of gentlemen, as their fathers bought up the advowsons formerly held by monasteries. With those advowsons came monastic tithes, yielding higher incomes to uphold their gentle status.

The dissolution of the monasteries effectively reversed the Gregorian reforms of the twelfth century. The laity reacquired much of the control over the church which they had lost in the twelfth century. By 1603, 1,031 out of 1,271 advowsons in the Diocese of Lincoln were in lay hands. Over the country as a whole, over half of advowsons probably remained in gentle hands from the sixteenth to the twentieth centuries.

It took a century after the Reformation for the clergy to become a graduate profession. In 1620 two-thirds of the clergy in the Diocese of Oxford were graduates; by 1640 virtually all were. If you were a graduate, the bishop would ordain you, your father would present you to the family living and the bishop would institute you to that living. Many clergy served as curates to a parochial incumbent before becoming one, although that was by no means always required. Incidentally, if the bishop owned the advowson, the clergyman was collated to the living rather than presented and instituted.

The Reformation opened the way for the development of the clerical dynasty. One such dynasty was the Rouse family of North Cornwall. Oliver Rouse, the civil war rector of Kilkhampton (Cornwall), was the father of Isaac Rouse, who was instituted to the living of Week St Mary in 1644. Isaac's son became vicar of North Petherwin, a daughter married the vicar of Stratton, and a granddaughter married John Turner, one of Isaac's successors at Week St Mary.

The incumbent stood at the centre of parish life. Before the Reformation, the term 'sir' was an honorific commonly applied to him. His benefice was freehold property, although inalienable. Once inducted, he could not easily be dismissed. He had a wide variety of duties. His primary function was spiritual: he was responsible for the cure of souls and the spiritual wellbeing of his parishioners. He ensured that there were regular services in the parish church; he baptized, married and conducted funeral services for his flock. The chancel, the glebe and the parsonage house were all his responsibilities.

He had to read proclamations from the pulpit. Occasionally he was expected to keep the parish bull. He chaired meetings of the vestry and nominated one of the two churchwardens. Sometimes he was much more involved than that: the churchwardens' accounts of Morebath (Devon) demonstrate the close involvement of its rector in the churchwardens' business.

The incumbent was expected to compile the parish register and send transcripts to the bishop. He attended visitations from bishops and archdeacons, answered visitation queries on the state of his parish and took the oaths of executors and administrators when required to do so. Poor relief was originally his responsibility, although from 1598 overseers undertook the routine tasks. He also took a leading role in the administration of parochial charities.

In return, the clergy were exempt from serving as parish officers, in the armed forces, or on juries. The privilege known as 'benefit of clergy' drastically reduced penalties imposed for any felonies. They could not be arrested in any civil suit while going about their spiritual duties. They were exempt from church rates, although liable to poor rates.

The income of incumbents was derived from tithes (discussed in Chapter 7), the glebe, surplice fees, mortuaries and other offerings. The 'great tithes' of corn and hay were frequently owned by impropriators: monastic owners of the rectory and their gentry successors. Between them, Elizabeth I and James I sold no fewer than 3,669 lots of impropriated parish tithes seized during the dissolution to the gentry.[5] Some purchasers extinguished tithes by purchasing both them and the land liable to pay them, but a third of tithes were owned by lay impropriators in the late eighteenth century.[6]

The vicars who actually served the cures in impropriated parishes frequently – but not invariably – relied on the small tithes. These were paid on a wide range of produce: for example, fleeces, livestock, apples and honey. They were difficult and expensive to collect; efficient collection demanded the local knowledge that only a resident curate could hope to possess. Tithing customs varied from parish to parish. At Laneast (Cornwall), even the small tithes had been impropriated; the tithe owner paid the curate £7 per annum. Small tithes sometimes formed a part of the Easter offering and may be recorded in Easter books (see Chapter 5).

Surplice fees were paid for marriages, burials and the churching of women, but rarely for baptisms. Amounts depended on local custom. Marriage fees generally amounted to a shilling or two, although sometimes they depended on social status. At Tregony (Cornwall), they could be as high as half a guinea 'according to the persons'. In Staffordshire, the fee for a marriage by licence was frequently double that for a marriage by banns.[7] A third of Cornish parishes made no charge for burials. Elsewhere, fees ranged from 4 pence in North Petherwin to 5 shillings, 'according to the person', at Tregony.[8]

'Churching' of women was a purification ceremony conducted after childbirth. In Cornwall, the standard fee in 1727 was 6 pence. However, the service gradually fell into disuse, although it is still printed in the *Book of Common Prayer*.

Mortuaries were payments made to incumbents upon the death of parishioners. In 1727 they were collected in about half of the parishes in Cornwall and attracted much opposition. Egloshayle's mortuaries were 'lost', while those of Paul were 'scrupled'. The Mortuaries Act of 1529 limited the amount that could be exacted, although its provisions were sometimes breached by local custom. After 1529, mortuaries were only payable in parishes where they had previously been customary. However, the poor were not liable.

Most rectories were endowed with glebe land which provided clergy with a substantial proportion of their income. Glebes are described in detail in glebe terriers. Over half the livings in early eighteenth-century Cornwall had less than 30 acres of glebe, although eight Cornish incumbents had over 100 acres. Originally, the incumbent was expected to farm his glebe himself. Ralph Josselin, rector of Earls Colne (Essex) in the mid-seventeenth century, has left us a detailed record of his farming routine.[9] As late as 1714, the rector of Ilmington (Warwickshire) was farming his glebe himself.[10] Increasingly, however, the glebe was let out. By the mid-eighteenth century, active participation in farming was seen as unbecoming to a clergyman. Shute Barrington, Bishop of Salisbury, warned his clergy that 'the habits of life in which the clergy are educated, and the important office they fill, are ill-suited to the occupation of a farmer.'[11]

The glebe included the parsonage house. Glebe terriers provide detailed descriptions of them. Parsonages were important: if the house was adequate, it enabled the incumbent to reside in his parish. Eighteenth-century parsonages, however, were increasingly seen as inadequate by status-conscious clergy with rising incomes. Tithe commutation gave a vast stimulus to the building of new parsonage houses, but these created a serious problem for the church in the twentieth century when they became far too expensive to maintain. Most are no longer occupied by incumbents.

The enclosure movement contributed substantially to the rise in clergy status. Enclosure added over 185,000 acres to glebes between 1757 and 1835. It enabled rectors to commute tithes for land. The favourable treatment given to clergy, combined with the increased profitability of enclosed lands, meant that enclosure could double incumbents' income. The rector of Hillington (Norfolk) observed that his predecessors had rarely received more than £200 from tithes. Enclosure gave him an income of about £500 'without any trouble & vexation by which it was before obtained'. In the twenty counties where enclosure was most prevalent, an average of almost 159 acres was added to the glebe.[12] Many incumbents were raised to gentry status, becoming increasingly differentiated from poor curates who were not entitled to tithe.

There was a huge disparity between the wealthiest and the poorest clergy, exacerbated by the enclosure movement. Tithe commutation was not possible for those clergy who owned no tithes. Disparities in clergy incomes became a major problem for the church. The early reformers had hoped to use at least some of the capital from the dissolved monasteries to improve the incomes of poorer livings, but the Tudors decided otherwise. The Interregnum regime did begin to introduce reforms but these were nipped in the bud at the Restoration. The clergy had to wait until 1704 for a monarch to act on the issue.

First fruits and tenths were, in origin, papal taxes on the incomes of all benefices. In 1523 Henry VIII seized them and redirected them into the Crown's coffers. In 1704, they were diverted into Queen Anne's Bounty. This fund purchased land in order to augment the glebes of poorer clergy.[13] Taxes paid by the wealthier clergy were used to support their poorer brethren. At Cheddleton (Staffordshire) the curate's stipend of £5 6s 8d was increased by rents totalling £23.

Sometimes the income of incumbents was supplemented by benefactors. At West Bromwich (Staffordshire), rents worth £32 13s 4d were in the hands of charity trustees in 1693. The incumbent was to be paid for Sunday sermons, providing the trustees thought the incumbent suitable.[14]

More than half the benefices in the mid-eighteenth century were worth less than £50.[15] The poorest clergy were forced to become pluralists, holding several poor livings at the same time in order to obtain a tolerably decent income. In Wiltshire it has been calculated that 124 of its 262 clergymen in 1783 were pluralists, 89 of necessity. Only 90 of its 232 parishes had resident incumbents, although a further 39 had resident stipendiary curates. Eighty more had an incumbent or curate living within 5 miles.[16] In 1808 some 60 per cent of livings in England and Wales had non-resident incumbents.

Not all clergy were incumbents. Many curates were employed to do the work of non-resident or pluralist incumbents. John Trelosek, 'capellanus' [chaplain], served at Ashburton (Devon) for thirty years in the late fifteenth century. Curates might also be employed to serve chapels of ease in large parishes. Sometimes they were allowed surplice fees and/or the small tithes; elsewhere, they were simply paid a stipend. Before the Reformation, chantry priests were expected to assist the incumbent in parochial duties. When chantries were abolished in 1547, the Mildenhall (Suffolk) churchwardens pointed out that their two chantry priests provided much-needed support to their parish priest.

Pre-Reformation unbeneficed clergy could find plenty of work. Parochial investment in religious services was at its height at the beginning of the sixteenth century. There was great demand for priests able to say mass for souls in purgatory. Guilds frequently had their own chaplains; the nine in Mildenhall could perhaps have provided work for two priests in addition to the two chantry priests. Priests were needed to read bede rolls, hear confessions and preach. One in eight of the auxiliary priests in the Diocese of Winchester earned their income from additional funds raised by churchwardens, over and above the official requirements of the church.[17]

After the Reformation, the inability of many incumbents to preach frequently led to the employment of a lecturer. In 1578 the municipal authorities in Kendal (Westmorland) resolved 'to provide and find a learned preacher ... to join with the vicar of the said church that by them two they may have every Sunday in the year a sermon to their great comfort and edifying.' Payments for such duties are frequently recorded in churchwardens' accounts.

The ordinations and institutions of clergymen were recorded in bishops' registers and are being recorded in the Clergy of the Church of England Database at www.theclergydatabase.org.uk. This covers the period from 1540 to 1835. After 1858, the easiest way to trace Anglican clergy is to consult the brief biographical notices in *Crockford's Clerical Directory*. The *Clergy List* provides similar listings between 1846 and 1899. For the period 1800–1840, reference may also be made to Joseph Foster's *Index ecclesiasticus ...* (Parker & Co., 1890). Post-Reformation clergy are likely to be listed in university registers.[18] A detailed guide to tracing Anglican clergy is provided by Peter Towey's *My Ancestor Was an Anglican Clergyman* (Society of Genealogists, 2006).

Incumbents' names constantly recur in most of the records to be discussed in this book. Those records also depended upon the efforts of parish officers. In terms of the records with which this book is concerned, the churchwardens and the overseers were the most important but the constables and the highway surveyors (or waywardens) also performed important roles. These officers were responsible either to the bishop or to Justices of the Peace. However, all were regarded as representatives of their parish and all needed the cooperation of the vestry.

The Vestry

Originally, churchwardens were appointed at annual meetings of householders. However, as the range of statutory duties grew under the Tudors and as scrutiny from county and central government increased, the inadequacies of parish meetings were increasingly felt. Parishes needed more than just their officers to govern themselves effectively. They also needed a governing body that could supervise them and could ensure that obligations set by statute and canon law were met.[19] Vestries increasingly supplied the need. They could impose rates and consequently became as indispensable to the parish as parliaments able to impose taxation were to the Crown.[20]

The vestry took its name from the room in the church where it met, where vestments were kept. The earliest mention that has been uncovered is in 1504,[21] although it may be that meetings were being held before that. Vestries gradually established themselves in the sixteenth and seventeenth centuries. Their constitution varied, depending upon local custom. At Kettering (Northamptonshire), all ratepayers could attend; usually, twenty to thirty did so. Elsewhere, vestries became self-selecting oligarchies or perhaps dependent for their membership on the ownership of particular properties. Parochial elites took charge of parish affairs and excluded the lower orders from participation. Even in Kettering, the parish elite probably had the final say in parish matters.

Membership of a select vestry was limited; at Pittington (Co. Durham), there were only twelve vestrymen. The select vestry there was first established in 1584:

> 'it is agreed by the consent of the whole parishe to electe and chuse out of the same xij men to order and define all common causes pertaining to the church, as shall appertaine to the profit and commoditye of the same, without molestation or troubling of the rest of the comon people.'

In towns, borough officers frequently played an important role. Tewkesbury (Gloucestershire) churchwardens presented their accounts 'in the parishe churche' to the 'bailiffs of Tewkesbury and to other the burgesies and commonaltie of the same towne there present'.

Select vestries developed in a variety of ways. 'Immemorial custom' was held to legalize the older ones. At Ashburton (Devon), 'immemorial custom' ruled. The 'eight men' were elected for life; four by manorial tenants, four by the burgesses. The vestry 'made ordinances about parish affairs, levied fines for their disobedience, fixed the salaries of minor church officials, represented the parish in outside business, and leased or enfeoffed church property.'

In London, there was a trend towards select vestries in the sixteenth century. At St Martin's in the Fields, churchwardens were elected 'by the consent will and agreement of the whole body of the parich' in 1546. By 1561 they were submitting their accounts to the 'masters' of the parish, and by the end of the sixteenth century a closed vestry was firmly established, only to be displaced when it was challenged as being 'wholly corrupt' in 1834.

Select vestries could be established by a bishop's faculty. Such faculties were common in London.[22] In Stepney, a select vestry was created by bishop's faculty in 1662 following irregularities in the elected vestry during the Interregnum. The vestry itself appointed new vestrymen. Some faculties merely confirmed an existing state of affairs; others aimed to settle discord between parishioners. All claimed to be in the interests of good governance.

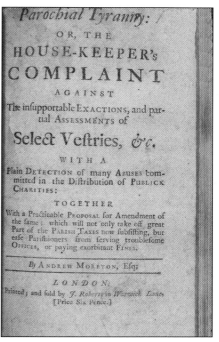

An eighteenth-century diatribe against select vestries.

Parliament was also responsible for creating select vestries. Church-building Acts, creating new parishes, were common in the eighteenth century, especially in London. They usually assumed that a select vestry would be established. When the parish of St Luke's was created from a part of the parish of St Giles Cripplegate in 1733, it was given a select vestry consisting of all those parishioners who had served as parish officers.

There was no general legislation affecting the constitution of vestries until 1818, when it was laid down that only ratepayers could attend and that a specified procedure had to be followed. The act legalized referendums. They had been known previously: in Woolwich, for example, polls were held between 1796 and 1804 on matters such as the salaries of the organist and the workhouse master. However, after 1818 polls could be demanded as a legal right. Outvoted parties in vestry meetings could insist on one. In Liverpool, there were no fewer than eight such referendums in 1832.

The term 'select vestry' acquired a different meaning under the Select Vestry Act of 1819. It authorized the election by all ratepayers of 'select vestries' to deal with Poor Law matters. Some 3,000 parishes chose to adopt its provisions. Such vestries ceased to meet after the 1834 Poor Law Act.

Many of the old London oligarchies continued for much of the nineteenth century. They took on the administration of many new services, and ultimately were transformed into the Metropolitan Borough Councils created in 1900. In the provinces, by comparison, oligarchies diminished in their powers until they were replaced by elected parish councils in 1894.

Vestries normally met at Easter for the election of churchwardens, as required by the canons. At the same meeting, or within a few weeks, they would also nominate overseers, for confirmation by Justices of the Peace. In September, they compiled lists of names from which Justices chose highway surveyors. Other meetings could also be held.

Vestries became 'the paternalistic embodiment of the parish, and custodians of its legal and financial interests.'[23] They established policy on such matters as the means of raising income, control over expenditure, church repairs, the relief of the poor, the management of church property and the appointment of lecturers. They exercised a variable amount of oversight over parish officers, who were also responsible to Justices of the Peace and bishops. Central government rarely interfered.

Sometimes vestries attempted to exercise oversight over their clergy. Churchwardens could present incumbents at visitations for misdemeanours; they could supplement their income, pay them for additional duties or appoint additional priests. Very occasionally, vestries acquired advowsons, giving them the right to appoint incumbents. The churchwardens of All Saints, Oxford, leased their advowson from the patron in 1538 so that they could 'prouyde procure and gette oon honeste priste of good name and fame to serve and have chardge of the cure of the said parisheners'. In London, thirteen vestries were appointing their own incumbents by the 1630s.

The legality of the vestry, however, was based on custom, not statute, and was open to doubt. The early seventeenth-century Laudian Royal Commission on fees posed a serious threat to any vestry that showed tendencies towards becoming a Presbyterian eldership, although it drew back from challenging the overall authority of select vestries. Even the legality of bishops' faculties could be challenged at common law.

Parish Officers

The vestry decided most parish business. However, churchwardens, overseers, constables and highway surveyors did most of the work. They were generally drawn from the parish elite: yeomen, substantial husbandmen and independent tradesmen, rather than servants or labourers. Gentlemen tended to avoid office as it was thought to lower their status.[24]

Office was a mark of social status. The Jacobean vicar of Stapleford Abbots (Essex) described the ideal:

'one that is able to do the King and country good service, we make him a constable, a sidesman, a head-borough, and at length a churchwarden: thus we raise him by degrees, we prolong his ambitious hopes, and at last we heap all our honours upon him.'[25]

Parish office offered humbler members of society the opportunity to exercise considerable power. Those appointed frequently held several different offices in the course of their lives. Well over 50 per cent of the constables in the parishes studied by Kent had also served as churchwardens. In boroughs, parish officers might also hold civic office: in late medieval Salisbury, fifteen churchwardens of St Edmunds also served as mayor.

Literacy and knowledge of the law were not required for appointment. In 1642, all constables in both Cheshire and Westmorland were illiterate, although the same could not be said of their contemporaries in Somerset where the illiteracy rate ran at 7 per cent. In 1657, Hertfordshire justices complained that illiterate constables were unfit to undertake their duties. In 1616, one Wiltshire constable had to walk 2 miles every time he received written warrants and precepts in order to have them read to him. Even then, he may not have understood them. Few parish officers had a sound understanding of legal principles, and very few would have had access to books such as William Lambarde's *The Duties of Constables, Borsholders, Tithingmen, and Such Other Lowe Ministers of the Peace* (1584).

Parish officers were rarely paid, despite their heavy responsibilities. Even when payment was made, it could be minimal: for example, the churchwardens of St Mary's, Bath occasionally received a stipend of 12 pence in the medieval period. The two Glastonbury (Somerset) churchwardens were paid a fee of 6s 8d in 1584. In the nineteenth century, more realistic payments were sometimes made. William Elkins, for example, agreed to serve as constable of Kettering (Northamptonshire) for 14 guineas in 1836.

The duties of parish officers involved considerable work, responsibility, and argument with neighbours. They worked closely together; indeed, the 1601 Poor Law specified that the officers were to meet once a month. In Thurgarton Hundred (Nottinghamshire), Justices of the Peace ensured that this happened by calling meetings themselves. The division of responsibilities between officers was frequently blurred: for example, constables and overseers both dealt with travellers and vagrants.

Given the lack of pay, it is not surprising that some of those elected tried to avoid serving. Sometimes an officer only agreed to serve on condition that he would not have to serve again. William Risdaile of Little Munden (Hertfordshire) agreed to serve as constable in 1639 'soe he may be excused for four years following'. The office of constable became unpopular in the 1630s when constables had to collect the controversial Ship Money instigated by Charles I to provide funding for naval forces. Office became even more unpopular after the Restoration, as Parliament expected parish officers to enforce an ever-increasing amount of repressive and distasteful legislation. Men were reluctant to undertake the onerous duties; the harsh punishments which could be imposed made them reluctant to report their neighbours' minor misdemeanours. Fines imposed on those who refused to serve provided a useful source of income to some parishes in London and other cities.

All parish offices could be served by deputy, and frequently were, especially in urban parishes. Officers had to serve until a replacement was found; if none could be found, the officer concerned could find himself obliged to continue in office, and might appeal to the Justices of the Peace to relieve him of his duties. A few people were exempt from serving, such as the clergy, Justices of the Peace, attorneys, militia men and dissenting ministers. Dissenters were permitted to appoint a deputy. Possession of a 'Tyburn ticket' also gave exemption: this was a certificate granted by a court for successful prosecution of an offender, and named after the place where executions took place in London.

CHURCHWARDENS

Most rural parishes had two churchwardens. Larger parishes might have more. In Manchester, there were eight: three for Manchester itself and one for each of the chapelries into which the parish was divided. By contrast, a few Cambridgeshire parishes had only one churchwarden at the end of the seventeenth century.

Churchwardens were chosen in a variety of different ways, depending on the custom of the parish concerned. The 1571 canons specified that they had to be chosen at Easter by minister and parishioners jointly. This was strengthened in 1604, when the minister was given the choice of one warden if he disagreed with his parishioners. The vestry made the choice of the other. Custom sometimes overrode the canons. The occupiers of particular properties might have a duty to serve by rotation or the retiring churchwardens might choose their successors. In Brighton, two churchwardens had to be 'substantial fishermen', and another a landsman. The borough council at Wells (Somerset) made the choice of St Cuthbert's churchwardens.

It was implicitly assumed that unpaid churchwardens had sufficient financial resources to cope with the cash-flow problems inherent in the system. It was also assumed that they were fit, as they had to undertake many journeys on horseback, sometimes spending nights away from home. The Prescot (Lancashire) churchwardens regularly found themselves summoned to attend the Consistory Court at Chester, Quarter Sessions at Wigan or Ormskirk, and Assizes at Lancaster. Summonses from such bodies had to be obeyed.

If a duly-elected churchwarden refused office, he could be penalized. At Stratton (Cornwall), 3s 4d was received in 1519 from 'Thomas Prieste for the refusing of the wardynshep'. In 1557, the parishioners of Mere (Wiltshire) decided that wardens should hold office for two years and that 13s 4d was the penalty for refusing office.

Women were infrequently chosen[26] unless they happened to own property that was on a rota from which churchwardens were selected. Such women were usually widows. Lady Isabel Newton served at Yatton (Somerset) in 1495; her gentle status overrode the fact that she was a woman. Her election enabled her to supervise the building of a new chapel where she and her husband were subsequently buried. At St Budeaux (Devon) it was the custom to choose a woman to serve as one of the two wardens, hence Widow Bragiton and Wm Rowe held office together in 1626.

Churchwardens were generally elected for one-year terms. Occasionally several terms were served but rarely more than two or three. Kümin has calculated that churchwardens in the areas he studied served for an average of two terms, not necessarily consecutively.[27] In the late seventeenth century, however, there was a trend towards longer terms of service in Cambridgeshire.[28] The record for length of service was probably held by John Saberton who served for twenty-five years at Peterborough from 1478.

Occasionally, an under-warden would be chosen who was to succeed as churchwarden in the following year. In the fifteenth century, the Salisbury (Wiltshire) church of St Edmunds had two senior wardens plus two juniors. The latter looked after the church's goods and ornaments, and took over from their seniors after a year in office. Such phased elections were normal in Hampshire[29] and helped to ensure the continuity of parish administration.

Churchwardens held – and continue to hold – the oldest ecclesiastical office available to laymen.[30] We have already seen how responsibility for church maintenance was transferred to the laity in the thirteenth century.

The administration of that responsibility necessitated the appointment of churchwardens. However, the church hierarchy did not create the office: rather, it was created by parishes responding to the financial demands of that hierarchy; a local response to the collective needs of the community.

The 'parish procurators' of Bristol in 1261 were the earliest-known holders of the office.[31] There were churchwardens at St Peter le Bailey, Oxford in 1270 and at St Mary's, Oxford in 1275. The Synod of Exeter in 1287 provided the earliest text outlining their duties.[32]

It was not until the sixteenth century that central government began to delegate secular responsibilities to churchwardens. When overseers of the poor were appointed, churchwardens became ex officio overseers. They also shared in some of the responsibilities of other parish officers. They were not, however, supposed to act until they had been sworn in at a visitation of the bishop or archdeacon.

Churchwardens required no education. In the sixteenth century, few could write their own accounts and scribes had to be employed. In Morebath (Devon) they were written by the incumbent. Maturity, and a certain social status, was expected. At St Mary's, Chester the average age of a churchwarden between 1560 and 1630 was 33.2, compared to 26.5 for sidesmen.[33] George Herbert wrote that 'the parson suffers not the place [of wardens] to be vilified or debased by being cast on the lower ranke of people, but invites and urges the best unto it.'[34]

Churchwardens served for a variety of different motives. All would have been proud of their parish; most would have wished to be involved in its governance and the promotion of its interests. The position demonstrated the attainment of a certain status in society. It also offered, in pre-Reformation days, a means of performing 'good works' and thus an expectation of a measure of salvation. Negatively, refusing office could mean payment of a hefty fine.

Originally, churchwardens were appointed to supervise the maintenance of the church and churchyard. They needed to keep an eye on the roof, the windows, the tower and the walls. They were responsible for their church's furnishings: the altar, the font, images, organs, pews, roods, bells and clocks. They levied rates and paid the church's bills. They collected money on charity briefs and administered bequests made to the parish. They provided the materials needed for worship. Pre-Reformation churchwardens devoted much of their effort to providing wax for 'lights' before images. Incense also had to be provided: it symbolized the prayers of the faithful rising to God, and cleansed the church of evil spirits and obnoxious smells.

After the Reformation, churchwardens provided wine and bread for communion; the plate (such as chalice and patten) needed for communion;

the books setting out the liturgy to be followed; the bible to be read during services; and the vestments needed by the priest. They allocated pews to parishioners. They also submitted regular presentments to bishops or archdeacons at visitations, reporting on the state of the fabric, the conduct of the priest and the morals of the parishioners. Archdeacons expected to view both an inventory of church goods and the churchwardens' accounts.

Under the Tudors, churchwardens' responsibilities were steadily extended. From 1538, they were supposed to ensure that the parish register of baptisms, marriages and burials was written up by the incumbent weekly, and they each kept one of the keys to the parish chest where the register was stored. A statute of 1552 enforced compulsory attendance at church and churchwardens were given the task of enforcement. They kept order during services, made sure that taverns were closed at service times, checked up on those who failed to attend, and excluded excommunicates. Their presentments dealt with such matters as slander, sexual misdemeanours, refusal to pay tithes and non-attendance at church. At Walton-on-the-Hill (Lancashire) the churchwardens regularly listed communicants at Easter, presumably with the intention of presenting those who failed to attend.

Churchwardens were required to enforce punishments imposed by the ecclesiastical courts. They levied penalties for eating flesh on fish days, for keeping unlicensed alehouses, for 'tippling' and drunkenness, for selling corn by wrong measures, and for a wide range of other misdemeanours.[35]

According to Burn, post-Reformation churchwardens were required to

'take care to have in the church a large bible, book of common prayer, book of homilies, a font of stone, a decent communion table, with proper coverings, the ten commandments set up at the east end, and other chosen sentences upon the walls, a reading desk, and pulpit, and chest for alms; all at the charge of the parish.'[36]

Successive Acts of Parliament associated them with other parish officers in dealing with such matters as poor relief and highway maintenance. They paid for the extermination of vermin. At Walton-on-the-Hill they were responsible for the maintenance of the school and served as school reeves.

Churchwardens had split loyalties: the Ordinary (the bishop) expected them to report to him but their fellow parishioners could also hold them to account, as could Justices of the Peace. The demands of government and local society could be in serious conflict and could place them in an invidious position. When William Wood, churchwarden of Prescot, travelled to Wigan to defend the parish against orders to provide for the poor, he found himself in prison for two days with a fee of £1 to pay for the privilege.

The churchwardens of Masham (Yorkshire) in 1571 found themselves caught between the irresistible demands of the archbishop and the incumbent to tear down their rood loft and images, and the demand of their neighbours, presented at the point of pikestaff and dagger, that the burning be halted.[37] Churchwardens could, however, be rewarded. If they presented a recusant for non-attendance at church, and he was convicted, the churchwarden was entitled to a reward of 40s, to be levied on the recusant's goods.

Churchwardens' views of their duties did not necessarily correspond with those of higher authorities. Puritan or Roman Catholic churchwardens could and did obstruct the intentions of government. Failure to present offenders might be due to social pressure, corruption, neighbourliness, friendship, pity, procrastination or just plain incompetence. Archbishop Neile's visitors in early seventeenth-century Lancashire complained of 'these wilful churchwardens [presumably Puritanically-minded] ... whom they could not get to present any' and thought that 'till some be exemplary punished ... the rest will never take care to discharge their duties and their othes.'[38] In 1680 the Bishop of Peterborough complained that 'defects can never be known by the presentments of the churchwardens'.

Churchwardens were regarded as the representatives of their parish and were expected to appear on their parish's behalf at ecclesiastical visitations and Quarter Sessions. They sometimes undertook extensive legal action on behalf of their parish. The Poor Law occasioned many disputes, but a wide range of other issues could also lead to court action. The Walton-on-the-Hill churchwardens were involved in a lengthy dispute with the mayor and corporation of Liverpool (which formed part of their parish) during the 1650s; they also undertook litigation against the Molyneaux family over a bad debt.

Churchwardens' activities cost money, recorded in their accounts. These therefore provide revealing insights into parochial life and will be considered in Chapter 3.

OVERSEERS

The church has always regarded the relief of the poor as a priority. The dissolution of the monasteries, which had been the most important institutional providers of poor relief, meant that the parishes became the front line for the church to fulfil its responsibilities. The government, however, had other priorities. 'Rogues and vagabonds' were seen as an increasing threat to society. Increasingly, that threat was met by turning to the parishes to provide poor relief and a measure of social control.

Initially this responsibility was laid on churchwardens, who, in 1536, were authorized to make regular collections for the poor. In Edward VI's reign, they were authorized to appoint parochial collectors for the same purpose. Overseers of the poor were first mentioned in legislation in 1572: their duty was to serve as alms collectors and to supervise the work of rogues and vagabonds. Finally, in 1598 and 1601, responsibility for poor relief was assigned to parish overseers. Between two and four overseers could be appointed, depending on the size of the parish.

Overseers were nominated by the parish but appointed by two Justices of the Peace, to whom they were expected to render accounts. Those nominated could only evade serving by paying a fine or finding a substitute. Roger Fowke, appointed as overseer for Gnosall (Staffordshire) in 1747, hired Richard Bernard to act for him. Women could be appointed in this role and in 1782 Margaret Reynolds served in Gnosall. Unlike most female overseers, she undertook the work herself rather than paying a man to do it.

Payment of overseers, until 1819, was technically illegal. However, William Startin was appointed as paid overseer of Gnosall in 1779. He had already acted for previous overseers. When payment was legalized, the number of paid overseers increased dramatically and by 1834 there were over 5,000.[39]

The author of *An Ease for Overseers of the Poore*, writing in 1603, argued that the 'office of overseer extendeth fare but it consisteth specially in taxing contributions for the relief of the poore and the discrete dispensation and ordering thereof'. Overseers were expected to assess and collect the poor rates, to relieve the poor, to set them to work, and to bind pauper children as apprentices. In many parishes they administered doles and other charities bequeathed for the poor. Parish chests are full of the records of overseers' activities. These will be discussed in Chapter 4.

In 1834 overseers lost most of their responsibilities to Poor Law Unions. However, they continued to help relieve the casual poor, to provide lodging in cases of 'sudden and urgent necessity', and to pay relief if directed to do so by the Guardians. They could still enforce maintenance payments and instigate removal orders; about 12,000 paupers were removed in 1907.[40] Overseers continued to levy poor rates until 1925, when the office was abolished.

CONSTABLES

A constable held the oldest parochial office, which only became overshadowed by the churchwarden and the overseer in the seventeenth century. He was originally appointed by the manorial court leet and was sometimes known as a borsholder or headborough; he acted as the village headman. In 1285 the Statute of Westminster recognized him as 'conservator of the peace'. When court leets ceased to meet, appointment might be made by the vestry. After 1662 appointments could be made by two Justices of the Peace. They usually allowed local custom to determine their choice. Nevertheless, a study of twenty-eight counties has shown that, in 1836, parish constables were still appointed by court leets in 63 per cent of petty sessional divisions.[41] The power of appointment was transferred to Justices of the Peace in 1842.

Women could be appointed, although they might then appoint a deputy to act on their behalf. Jane Kitchen, for example, served as constable at Upton (Nottinghamshire) in 1644, following her husband's death. She hired William Chappell to help her fulfil the duties of the office.

Constables, like churchwardens, had dual loyalties. Their prime duty was to execute the warrants of the local Justices of the Peace. They were underlings of both the High Constable of the Hundred and of the Lord Lieutenant. During the civil war they became factotums for whichever party had the nearest garrison. They worked closely with churchwardens and overseers. Constables were concerned with the restraint of conflict among neighbours, rather than the enforcement of impersonal regulations. Like the churchwarden, the constable was likely to be more concerned with his neighbours' interests than with those of the Crown. He would be blamed by his neighbours if he enforced collection of unpopular taxes like Ship Money but blamed by his superiors if he did not:

The justices will set us by the heels
If we do not as we should
Which, if we perform, the townsmen will storm,
Some of them hang's if they could[42]

The constable maintained the stocks, the pillory, the village lock-up and the parish armour. He kept the parish's weights and measures. He arrested offenders and raised the hue and cry. He escorted offenders to appear before Justices, and paupers being removed from his parish. He exercised oversight over vagrants, servants, alehouse-keepers, victuallers and recusants. In cities, he kept 'watch and ward' at night, guarding the city gates. He collected county rates, together with national taxes such as the 1513 poll tax, the subsidy, Ship Money in the 1630s, Parliament's 'monthly pay' and excise taxes during the civil war, the late seventeenth-century hearth tax and the eighteenth-century land and window taxes. He levied purveyance, meeting costs when royalty visited. He provided postmasters with horses when required. The demands of saltpetre men had to be met. The constable

The stocks at Keevil (Wiltshire), maintained by the parish constable.

raised the militia, impressed soldiers and lit beacons when necessary. In time of plague, he isolated those who were infected. He claimed his expenses, either from those he arrested or by levying a rate on parishioners.

A number of duties derived from the constable's original function as a manorial officer. He might be expected to keep the village bull (although sometimes that was the incumbent's task), to maintain pinfolds and hedges, to guard crops from both domestic and wild animals, and to undertake other agricultural tasks.

Constables were entitled to call upon the assistance of householders when needed. In 1605 the Pattingham (Staffordshire) manorial court ordered householders to have 'a sufficient club' to provide assistance if needed.[43] There were dangers in serving the office: the constable of

29

Woodford Bridge (Essex) was awarded 4s 6d in 1832 as compensation for having every window in his house broken.

The constable spent much of his time liaising with high constables, coroners, Justices of the Peace, and the collectors of county rates and national taxes. His duties took him out of his parish more frequently than other officers. The constable of Hooton Pagnell (Yorkshire) at the end of the eighteenth century was required to attend Quarter Sessions, Petty Sessions, Brewster Sessions and the Assizes. He summoned jurors and made presentments on a wide range of topics (presentments are discussed in Chapter 10). Constables are likely to be listed among Quarter Sessions records.

During the eighteenth century, duties increased, administration became more professional, and men became increasingly reluctant to serve. Those who did became increasingly ineffective. Payment of constables became common until it was stopped by a Poor Law Commissioners' ruling in 1836. Prosecutions plummeted.[44] By then, the position was increasingly being seen as obsolescent. In London, parish constables had already been abolished when the Metropolitan Police Service was established in 1829. In the provinces, they were gradually replaced with professional police forces following the County Police Act of 1839 and abolished in 1856.

No adequate history of parish constables has been written. However, for the early seventeenth century, see the indispensable:
• Kent, Joan R., *The English Village Constable 1598–1642: A Social and Administrative Study* (Clarendon Press, 1986).

HIGHWAY SURVEYORS

Parishes had always been responsible for maintaining their roads. The Tintinhull (Somerset) churchwardens spent 3s 5d on road stones as early as 1437. The Highways Act of 1555, which created the position of highway surveyor, gave custom statutory force. Surveyors were to be chosen by churchwardens, constables and other parish notables. A 1691 Act required parishes to nominate ten of 'the most sufficient inhabitants', from whom Justices of the Peace had to choose. Those nominated rarely had any knowledge of surveying or engineering. Payment was permitted: in Camberwell (Surrey) from 1781 the office was held for many years by successive members of two families, who were paid £50 per annum.

The surveyor's work was directed by Justices at their special Highway Sessions. The Justices decided where repairs or road-widening were needed or where roads should be closed. They received the surveyor's four-monthly presentments and audited his accounts, although the vestry also expected to see them.

Parishioners assisted surveyors. The 1555 Act required everyone who owned a ploughland or a plough to provide 'one wain or cart furnished after the custom of the country with oxen, horses or other cattle and all other necessaries meet to carry things convenient for that purpose, and also two able men with the same'. Other householders and cottagers served as labourers or sent someone in their stead. They were required to work for four consecutive days, subsequently six, in each year. Fines for default could be imposed. After 1670, an exemption fee of 1s 6d could be paid.

Surveyors directed statutory labour. They collected defaulters' fines and, subsequently, exemption fees; they also gave peremptory orders for the removal of obstructions in the highway. A parish's failure to keep roads in repair meant presentment at Quarter Sessions and a fine, with surveyors expected to collect the fine.

Parish Servants

Most parishes had a variety of paid servants, such as the parish clerk, the sexton, the sidesmen, the verger, the bellman, the organist, the dog-whipper and the field master. The vestry clerk was an eighteenth-century innovation. The activities of these servants are frequently detailed in parish records.

Parish Clerks

Parish clerks held a pre-Conquest office. They were originally regarded as clergymen in minor orders. A twelfth-century papal decretal required a priest to have 'a fitting and honest clerk' to assist him. He was expected to sing (especially the psalms), to read the epistle, and to teach. In the thirteenth century most were adolescents, usually chosen by incumbents from among parishioners, and frequently preparing for ordination. By the sixteenth century, the position was usually held for life.

The canons of 1604 required the parish clerk 'to be of honest conversation and sufficient for his reading writing and also for his competent skill in singing, if it may be.' After the Restoration, he was usually a layman.

The medieval clerk served at mass, accompanied the priest on pastoral visits, distributed holy bread and carried the holy water bucket, frequently being known as the 'water carrier'. Post-Reformation clerks continued to assist the clergy in conducting services, leading congregational singing and responses, perhaps reading the lessons (although not the prayers), making announcements and acting as verger. They frequently occupied a seat below the minister's desk. At Great Budworth (Cheshire), the new pulpit erected in 1737 had 'One reading desk for the parson & another for the Clark under or below the said pulpit.'

Twin reading desks at Mildenhall (Wiltshire): one for the rector and one for the parish clerk.

The parish clerk in a double-decker pulpit, as pictured by Hogarth.

A 1666 parish register entry from Buxted (Sussex) records the burial of Richard Basset, 'the old clarke of this parish', colourfully describing his performance in services: 'his melody warbled forth as if he had been thumped on the back by a stone.' He was probably better than another parish clerk whose singing was described as 'squeakinge like a gelded pigg'!

In addition to his liturgical duties, the parish clerk might also be expected to wash the surplices and table linen, to clean the plate, to maintain and ring the bells and to wind the clock. He might teach in school. At St Petrock's, Exeter he played the organ. According to Dr Johnson, 'the parish clerk should be a man who is able to make a will, or write a letter for anybody in the parish.' Sometimes he wrote the parish register (despite the injunction requiring incumbents to do so).

Payment varied. Some parish clerks conducted their own collections while others were paid a salary. The Mere (Wiltshire) clerk was paid £8 per annum in 1579. He did well. Cornish clerks were paid an average of about £2, although the amount varied from 7 shillings in St Juliot to £5 7s 6d at St Stephen by Saltash.

Salaried parish clerks sometimes also took a collection. At St Neots (Cornwall), a fixed amount had to be paid by each inhabitant: 2 pence by cottagers and a groat for each tenement.[45] At Hamstall Ridware (Staffordshire), clerks took some payments in kind; for example, two eggs at Easter from each of the larger farms.[46] Additional duties sometimes involved additional payments. At Betley (Staffordshire), the clerk received 1s 6d for every marriage by banns and 2s 6d for every marriage by licence. Burials and churchings also yielded fees.

Parish clerks are discussed in the introduction to:
• Legg, J. Wickham, ed. *The Clerk's Book of 1549.* (Henry Bradshaw Society, 1903).
See also:
• Ditchfield, P.H. *The Parish Clerk.* (Methuen & Co., 1907).

VESTRY CLERKS

The growth of parish business in the eighteenth century led some energetic vestries to employ a salaried vestry clerk. This gave them much greater control over parish business. At Woolwich in 1715 the vestry clerk attended all meetings of parish officers, drew up accounts, rate lists, registers of apprentices and the like, and acquired full knowledge of all parish business. Gradually the practice of employing such clerks spread into the provinces. In 1827 the remote parish of Shobrooke (Devon) appointed two vestry clerks who were 'to pay the poor, and keep the accounts'; they were paid a salary of £7 10s each.

THE SEXTON

Most parishes had a sexton, although sometimes the office was held in conjunction with other positions: at Old Warden (Bedfordshire) the terrier of 1727 states that 'the Offices of Clerk & Sexton are in one Person appointed by ye Vicar'. His primary duty was to dig graves. He also cleaned the church, opened pews, provided candles and other necessaries, washed the linen, attended Divine Service, kept out excommunicated persons and prevented any disturbance in the church. Walter Antony received 10 shillings as sexton at Ashburton (Devon) in 1513–14; he was also paid 4s 5d for looking after the clock and bells, 4 shillings for ringing the bell, 2s 4d for mending vestments and 2 pence for cleaning the church gutters. His contemporary at St Mary at Hill (London) was paid rather more. He had 40 shillings per annum but also undertook more responsible duties such as collecting the church rents and 'engrossing' the accounts.

The sexton probably charged fees for grave-digging not mentioned in most churchwardens' accounts. A rare schedule of sexton's fees from Chelmsford (Essex) in 1614 shows that 8 pence was charged for a burial in the churchyard without a coffin, reduced to 6 pence if the deceased was a child; a burial with a coffin cost 2 shillings. These fees seem to have been additional to any charges made by the churchwardens.

BEDESMEN

A bedesman was a pre-Reformation pensioner obligated to pray for the dead. The Ashburton (Devon) bedesman walked the streets with a bell, calling on parishioners to join him in his prayers. He assisted the sexton in cleaning the church and cemetery. In Hythe (Kent), Thomas the bedesman was paid 16s for watching the organ: he was evidently a night watchman and slept in the church, since he was given a gown worth 4 shillings 'for lying in the church'.

BEADLES

In the eighteenth and nineteenth centuries the beadle played an equivalent role, at least in the metropolis. He provided menial assistance to parish officers, perhaps collecting the poor rate, arresting vagrants, or 'crying' vestry meetings. Frequently he kept order during services. At Cirencester (Gloucestershire), he prevented parents bringing to church 'such of their children as either by crying or other noise shall be any disturbance in divine service'.

ORGANISTS AND SINGERS

Parishes with organs required an organist. They also required an organ-blower. Not every church could afford music but St Mary at Hill (London) had an organ from as early as 1479. Its early sixteenth-century organist, John Norfolk, probably taught choirboys, as money was expended to provide 'Norfolk's children' with surplices. St. Giles Cripplegate was given its organ in 1672. The task of playing it was given to the sexton; he 'to play upon it, Sundayes, Holy dayes, Wensdayes, Fridayes and Lecture Dayes, and his Sextons place to be voyd if he shall faile in any part of his duty.' At Ashburton (Devon), William Whyte was paid 3s 4d per year between 1546 and 1552 'for performing the office of cantor in the choir'.

Dog-whippers

There must have been times when the singing could not be heard for the noise of dogs barking. Parishioners were frequently accompanied by dogs when they came to church, and dog-whippers were appointed to control them. Between 1547 and 1621 the churchwardens of St Nicholas, Warwick, regularly named its dog-whipper in their accounts. Sometimes dog-whippers' duties extended beyond dogs. At Prestwich (Lancashire), George Grimshaw received 13s a year plus a new coat 'for his trouble and pains in wakening sleepers in ye church, whipping out dogs, keeping children quiet and orderly, and keeping ye pulpit and church walks clean'.

Sidesmen

Larger parishes appointed sidesmen (originally known as synodsmen or questmen). After 1662, four sidesmen were regularly appointed to assist churchwardens at St Edmund, Salisbury. Sidesmen acted as general assistants to the churchwardens, attending visitations and witnessing presentments. The 1604 canons required them, together with the churchwardens, to 'diligently see that all the parishioners duly resort to their church upon all Sundays and holy days … and none to walk or stand idle or talking in the church, or in the churchyard, or in the church porch, during that time.' At St Michael's in Bedwardine, Worcester their duties were defined as 'to be joined with the said wardens for placing of seats, things to be done about the church lands, and necessary affairs about the church'. A sarcastic poem in the parish books of Childwell (Lancashire) outlines sidesmens' supposed duties:

> To ken and see and say nowt,
> To eat and drink and pay nowt,
> And when the wardens drunken roam,
> Your duty is to see them home.

Accounts make it clear that the accusations in this poem were not always false. Many record payments for wining and dining on official occasions.

Parish Records

All of these officers and servants are mentioned in parish records. Parish officers in particular created many records. Sometimes these were kept in a very higgledy-piggledy manner. The same book might be used for a variety of different purposes. The medieval church book of All Saints, Bristol includes a few parish ordinances, a list of parish benefactors and their gifts, inventories of church goods for 1395 and 1469, a list of early fifteenth-century churchwardens, abstracts of churchwardens' accounts, and other memoranda.[47] A later book from Shobrooke (Devon) includes the accounts of surveyors, constables and the parish 'stock' (a charity for the poor), together with burials 1763–94, notes on briefs 1678–83, a list of parish officers 1763–94 and the inventory of a pauper's goods taken in 1690. Parish registers can go far beyond their ostensible subjects. A huge range of information can be found in them; so much so that Steve Hobbs has devoted an entire volume to *Gleanings from Wiltshire Parish Registers* (Wiltshire Record Society, 63. 2010). It is clearly necessary to consult the whole range of parish records in order to be sure of finding every titbit of information relating to, for example, the church bells or the apprenticing of paupers.

The church building itself could be described as a parish record. The various styles used, the images (or remains of them), the monuments, the furnishings, the setting; all can provide valuable information concerning the history of the parish. However, that is another book. The aim here is to discuss the diversity of books and papers formerly stored in parish chests, focusing primarily on the period between the fifteenth and the nineteenth century when the parish was all-important in the life of society.

Much has been lost through the vicissitudes of time. Damp and vermin have wrought much destruction, as have wars and general human carelessness. As recently as 1940 the wealth of medieval and later records possessed by St Nicholas, Bristol, was destroyed by a German bomb. It is fortunate that, in the mid-fifteenth century, Sir Thomas Norman had copies made of the accounts of St Mary's, Sandwich (Kent). They record that when the French sacked the town in 1456, they bore away a book 'where yn was conteynyd the a counties of the saiyd chyrche of a xij yere afore passid or more'. Many churchwardens were aware of the need to preserve their documents; indeed, some were deliberately made with posterity in mind. We must be grateful that many parish chests were strong enough to keep out the damp and the rats, and that so much material has survived as a result.

The Parish Chest

The earliest parish chests may date back to the eleventh century or even earlier. In 1166, a royal mandate instructed parishes to provide chests in which the faithful could place their offerings to support crusade in the Holy Land. A century later, in 1287, the Synod of Exeter ordained that every church should have its chest for books and vestments. Cromwell's 1538 injunctions regarding the safe-keeping of parish registers are well known: every parish was to provide 'one sure coffer with two lockes and keys whereof the one to remayne with you [the incumbent], and the other with the said wardens.' The 1604 canons repeated the injunction: 'the Churchwardens … shall provide one sure coffer with three locks and keys, whereof the one to remain with the Minister and the other two with the Churchwardens severally.'

Parish chests pre-date the earliest-known parish records, although it is clear that their existence reflects the increasing amount of paperwork involved in parish government. Most records stored in them in the medieval period have been lost. Much was destroyed during the Reformation including, for example, the bede rolls recording the names of the parish dead who were to be regularly prayed for, and the numerous service books

The parish chest at Steeple Ashton (Wiltshire).

The parish chest at Histon (Cambridgeshire). (Courtesy of Dr David Oates)

required for conducting Catholic liturgy. The reformers emptied parish chests of the wealth of metalwork and rich fabrics they contained. Cromwell's injunctions gave the chests a new purpose, although of course much has also been lost since the sixteenth century.

Parish chests can still be seen in most of our older parish churches. The earliest were hollowed out of tree trunks with an axe. These dug-outs are clumsy and weighty, with limited storage capacity despite their size. In the late thirteenth century joiners learned how to make chests from boards and subsequent centuries saw further improvements. Churchwardens' accounts are likely to record expenses in relation to chests: at Ashburton (Devon), for example, 8d was spent on making a key for the chest in 1484–5. Churchwardens frequently had their names or initials inscribed on new chests. At Raglan (Monmouthshire), the date '1677' is deeply cut into the wood, together with the initials 'W.G.', 'L.S.', and 'R.P.' The latter may stand for Raglan parish.

Seventeenth-century chests became increasingly ornate, although, subsequently, utilitarianism became the norm. Churchwardens needed adequate storage to hold the increasing quantity of paper generated by the administration of the Poor Law. The Registration Act of 1812 required 'dry, well painted iron chests' for the safe custody of the new baptism and burial registers. In 1813 the Sheepstor (Devon) churchwardens' accounts record

'Sundry charges to the Revd Mr Hunt for the Iron chist' amounting to almost £8.[48] These chests were dry in every sense; i.e. not very interesting.

For a recent study of Suffolk chests see:

• Sherlock, David, *Suffolk Church Chests.* (Suffolk Institute of Archaeology, 2007).

Tracing Parish Records

Most parish records are held in local record offices, although church safes still hold recent records. Stray records can sometimes be found among diocesan and Quarter Session records. Others are held by The National Archives at www.nationalarchives.gov.uk, the British Library at searcharchives.bl.uk, among the archives of universities and colleges and in other record offices. A union catalogue of record office archives is provided by:

• A2A: Access to Archives
  www.nationalarchives.gov.uk/a2a

For records from the capital, see:

• AIM25: Archives in London and the M25 area
  www.aim25.ac.uk

University and college archives are listed at:

• Archives Hub
  http://archiveshub.ac.uk/search/search.html

The websites of individual record offices have catalogues of their own collections, which do not necessarily duplicate these two union catalogues. Record office websites are listed at:

• Archon Directory
  www.nationalarchives.gov.uk/archon

Latin and Palaeography

Once records have been found, they need to be read. That may be easier said than done, especially in the case of older documents. Handwriting has changed over the centuries; therefore archaic hands have to be learned. Sometimes Latin was used rather than English. These problems should not deter the keen researcher. Scribes intended their writings to be read, so the difficulties should be surmountable. A number of aids to palaeography are available. Good online tutorials in both handwriting and Latin are provided by:

• Reading Old Documents
  www.nationalarchives.gov.uk/records/reading-old-documents.htm

The best guide to the Latin used in local records is:
- Stuart, Denis. *Latin for Local and Family Historians: A Beginner's Guide* (Phillimore, 1995).

For handwriting, an excellent introduction is provided by:
- Marshall, Hilary. *Palaeography for Family and Local Historians*. 2nd ed. (Phillimore, 2010).

Further Reading

There are a number of excellent modern studies of the role of the parish. For the medieval parish, see:
- Burgess, Clive & Duffy, Eamon, eds. *The Parish in Late Medieval England: Proceedings of the 2002 Harlaxton Symposium.* (Shaun Tyas, 2006).
- French, K., Gibbs, G.G. & Kümin, B., eds. *The Parish in English Life 1400–1600.* (Manchester University Press, 1997).
- French, Katherine L. *The People of the Parish: Community Life in a Late Medieval English Diocese.* (University of Pennsylvania Press, 2001).
- Kümin, Beat A. *The Shaping of a Community: The Rise and Reformation of the English Parish, c.1400–1560.* (Scolar Press, 1996).

For the parish in more recent centuries, see:
- Bettey, J.H. *Church and Community: The Parish Church in English Life.* (Moonraker Press, 1979).
- Snell, Keith D.M. *Parish and Belonging: Community, Identity and Welfare in England and Wales, 1700–1950.* (Cambridge University Press, 2006).

The classic study of documents from the parish chest is:
- Tate, W.E. *The Parish Chest: A Study of the Records of Parochial Administration in England*. 3rd ed. (reprint) (Phillimore, 1983).

For a focus on specifically ecclesiastical records, see:
- Bettey, J.H. *Church and Parish: An Introduction for Local Historians.* (B.T. Batsford, 1988).

Nineteenth-century sources are discussed in:
- Dunning, R.W. 'Nineteenth-Century Parochial Sources', in Baker, Derek, ed. *The Materials, Sources and Methods of Ecclesiastical History*. Studies in Church History, 11 (Ecclesiastical History Society, 1975), pp.301–08.

For local government history, the essential text is still:
- Webb, Sidney & Webb, Beatrice. *English Local Government from the Revolution to the Municipal Corporations Act: The Parish and the County.* (Longmans Green & Co., 1906).

Typical parish records are printed in:
- Purvis, J.S., ed. *Tudor Parish Documents of the Diocese of York: A Selection* (Cambridge University Press, 1948).

Digitized images of parish records, with various research guides, can be consulted at:

- London Lives 1690 to 1800: Crime, Poverty and Social Policy in the Metropolis
  www.londonlives.org

Researchers need some knowledge of parish law. See:

- Burn, Richard. *The Justice of the Peace and Parish Officer*. 7th ed. 3 vols., 1762. (There are many other editions.)
- *The Compleat Parish Officer*. 7th ed. 1734 (reprinted Wiltshire Family History Society, 1996).
- Holdsworth, W.A. *The Handy Book of Parish Law*. 1859. (reprinted Wiltshire Family History Society, 1995).

Historic parishes are mapped by:

- Kain, Roger J.P. & Oliver, Richard. *Historic Parishes of England and Wales: An Electronic Map of Boundaries Before 1850 with a Gazetteer and Metadata* (History Data Service, 2001).

There are many published editions of parish records, especially churchwardens' accounts, but also vestry minutes, settlement examinations and other documents. Some are cited in subsequent chapters. Many older works have been digitized and are available online. See:

- Internet Archive
  www.archive.org
- Open Library
  http://openlibrary.org
- Google Books
  http://books.google.com
- Family History Books
  http://books.familysearch.org
- Hathitrust Digital Library
  babel.hathitrust.org
- World Cat
  http://www.worldcat.org

Chapter 3

VESTRY MINUTES AND OFFICERS' ACCOUNTS

T he parish was governed by the vestry. Its minutes provide much useful information. So do the accounts of parish officers.[1] These are sources of first importance for both local and ecclesiastical historians, and will be discussed here, apart from the accounts of overseers which will be considered in Chapter 4.

Vestry Minutes

The vestry was concerned with most issues of parish governance. Parish officers worked closely with it and frequently took orders directly from it. The vestry's responsibilities are reflected in their minutes. It appointed or nominated parish officers, together with servants such as dog-whippers and sextons. It approved church rates and the accounts of churchwardens; it probably scrutinized glebe terriers before they were sent off to the Diocesan Registry. Most major decisions in the parish came before the vestry, despite the fact that parish officers bore legal responsibility for their execution. Church fabric, the parish armour and poor relief were just a few of the matters that came within its purview. In practice, vestries exercised a veto over the actions of parish officers, since the latter needed their support.

Vestries could also be interested in wider issues. In 1811, the vestry of St Olave Hart Street (London) petitioned Parliament against 'the claims of Roman Catholics to unlimited admission not only to Offices of High Trust & Power, but even unto the Legislature itself'.

Most surviving vestry minutes date from the eighteenth and nineteenth centuries. Earlier decisions may be recorded in churchwardens' accounts. In order to gain the fullest picture of parish activities, it is necessary to consult vestry minutes and accounts in conjunction with each other. The topics they deal with will therefore be considered below together.

Typically, the minutes of a vestry meeting record the parish, the date and the names of those attending. Usually they record specific decisions, such as the setting of a rate or the repair of fabric. Appointments and/or nominations of parish officers are frequently recorded in minutes. Reports from parish officers and others and correspondence received may also be minuted. Sometimes officers' accounts are included.

Minutes rarely reflect the ebb and flow of debate at meetings, although tensions may be recorded. For example, the Gnosall (Staffordshire) minute book was 'snatched away' by Edward Millington as the parishioners were signing it after a 1717 meeting; he 'refused to suffer ye parishners to subscribe their names'.

Accounts

Vestry minutes record the decisions and policies of the parish. The accounts of officers record what actually happened. Both reflect the responsibilities of the local community in maintaining their church. The origins of churchwardens' accounts can be traced to episcopal statutes. The statutes of Bishop Quivel of Exeter, issued in 1287, directed that the 'custodians' of parishes' should render every year a faithful account of the stock of the churches' to the Archdeacon.[2]

The earliest extant accounts known are those of Wigton (Cumberland) for 1328–9. The accountant acted not just as churchwarden but also as an agent for the rector, gathering his tithes and rents as well as the income of the church.[3] Surviving accounts are scarce for the fourteenth and fifteenth centuries. More survive from the early modern period. By the nineteenth century they are available for the majority of parishes.

Burn declared that 'it is most convenient, that every parish act there be entred in the parish book of accounts, and every man's hand consenting to it be set thereto; for then it will be a certain rule for the churchwardens to go by.'[4] His words suggest that he was conflating churchwardens' accounts with vestry minutes; certainly many parish books do this, for example, those of Stratford on Avon (Warwickshire) and St Columb (Cornwall). Similarly, many churchwardens' accounts record the income and expenditure of other officers. In smaller parishes, they may cover all income and expenditure. Elsewhere, there could be four or more sets of accounts: those of each of the officers, plus accounts for any separate fund(s). There is no way of knowing what proportion of the budget was actually recorded in accounts, or whether income raised for a particular purpose was necessarily spent in that way. In 1569/70, for example, the Lambeth parish officers used highway funds to pay for the eradication of vermin.

Medieval scribes frequently used separate parchment rolls for each year's account. Subsequently, paper books were used instead as scribes found rolls difficult to handle. Accounts written in books are generally more consistent in format, as scribes could easily see how they had previously been compiled. Double-entry book-keeping was rarely used before the seventeenth century. Accounts were usually kept annually, although other periods are known. Most follow a common pattern, commencing with a statement of the accounting period, perhaps the names of the accountants, the balance from the previous accounting period, the 'charge' (individual items of income), followed by the 'discharge' (individual items of expenditure). Then comes the balance, the acquittal of officers and notes on any sums still due or in the hands of others.

Particular items could be heavily abbreviated. In 1580–81, for example, the Kilmington (Devon) churchwardens reported the receipt of 46s from 'the bocke of ratmente for the churche', without any details of the ratepayers.

Sometimes accounts were written up from rough notes; that is evident, for example, from the church book of St Ewen's, Bristol.[5] At All Saints, Bristol, both the rough notes and the final accounts survive for the 1460s and 1470s. They enable us to see how heavily summarized the final accounts are, and how much is omitted. The purpose of accounts was not always just to exonerate the accountants at the audit or visitation. Sometimes they were commemorative, celebrating the achievements of churchwardens and consequently perhaps omitting much incidental detail.

Accounts required consent of the parish. It was therefore important that illiterate parishioners could understand what was being done in their names. The Morebath (Devon) accounts were written to be read aloud to parishioners. At Banwell (Somerset), 8 pence was paid 'for reading of the book of accounts'. Accounts had to be dictated to the scribe by the churchwardens, transcribed, recited to the parishioners and approved by them. The reading of churchwardens' accounts became a re-enactment of the financial events of the previous year.

Early accounts are not necessarily easy to read or understand. Handwriting may be appalling; a fact recognized by the vestry at Feniton (Devon) who thought that the outgoing wardens' accounts were 'so fowle that they thought not fit to have it ingrossed upon this booke'. Christopher Trichay, the vicar of Morebath (Devon), had a particularly distinctive and almost illegible hand which resulted in historians misreading a particularly significant entry. When correctly read, the entry revealed that the parish had paid for five young men to join the rebels during the 1549 Prayer Book Rebellion. On the other hand, some accounts reveal superb penmanship and are beautifully inscribed.

Words can sometimes be mystifying or misleading. For example, the 'daine Ruler' was paid a shilling at Harford (Devon) in 1697 and his compatriot, the Daynruler, was given wine valued at 1s 6d at Sheepstor (Devon) in 1762. Both scribes were referring to the rural dean, who inspected the churches in his deanery every year.[6] Glossaries are frequently included in editions of churchwardens' accounts, some of which are listed below. It may also be useful to consult James Halliwell-Phillipps' *A Dictionary of Archaic & Provincial Words, Obsolete Phrases, Proverbs, & Ancient Customs from the Fourteenth Century* (10th ed., 2 vols, John Russell Smith, 1887).

Medieval accounts were frequently written in Latin. Roman numerals continued to be used into the seventeenth century and sometimes later. The early churchwardens' accounts of St Edmunds, Salisbury were engrossed in Latin on rolls but transcribed in English into the church 'journal'. The scribe decided the format of accounts. Record-keeping was determined primarily by local priorities, despite the fact that bishops and archdeacons took an interest in what parishes were doing. Parish records began as a means of satisfying ecclesiastical authority; however, they rapidly became important as expressions of community concerns and priorities.

Early accounts were frequently written by paid scribes, who sometimes recorded the payment of their own fees. Between 1479 and 1580 there were ten different scribes in Ashburton (Devon), some of them attorneys. At St Michael's, Spurriergate, York, the accounts between 1518 and 1548 seem to be in the hand of Thomas Wyrral; he did the work for all forty-one churchwardens who served during those three decades.

Before the Reformation, the annual audit was made at various times of the year. The financial year frequently ran from 25 March but at Ashburton (Devon) the year commenced on 6 May; at Halesowen (Worcestershire) on 29 September. Most accounts covered a whole year but that was not always the case: one set of accounts from St Andrew Hubbard, Eastcheap (London) covered five years, from 1460 to 1465. Elizabethan Poor Law legislation prompted a general move to auditing at Easter.

Churchwardens were required to render 'a just account of such money as they have received, and also what particularly they have bestowed in reparations and otherwise, for the use of the church.' Receipts were supposed to be produced for all amounts over 40s. Sometimes these survive. Among the Tavistock (Devon) parish records are twenty-five receipts from 1657–8 giving the names of tradesmen who undertook masonry, carpentry and other tasks. These may well have been checked and expenses questioned, as audit was far from being a formality. Parishes sometimes appointed auditors to assist them: at St Andrew Hubbard, Eastcheap (London), four were appointed in 1509–10.[7]

Auditing did not always go smoothly: the six men of Morebath (Devon) 'cowd not make their cownt perfect' on at least one occasion during the Reformation years. In 1746 the Wimbledon (Surrey) vestry ordered the surveyors 'to apply to the next bench of justices, for a warrant of distress' in order to get a previous surveyor's accounts passed. It was not only the vestry that had to be satisfied. Churchwardens had to produce their accounts before their Archdeacon, and the secular officers had to satisfy Justices of the Peace.

Accounts are far from being a complete record of parish affairs; they do not necessarily record all financial transactions. In Steeple Ashton (Wiltshire), accounts frequently only record totals of income and expenditure. Even when the record is more detailed, gifts such as food and drink on perambulations or church decorations at festivals might escape notice. Collections were not necessarily recorded if all the money collected was spent on its declared object. We have already seen that sextons' fees may not have been recorded at all. However, the fact that an activity was not recorded in accounts does not mean that it did not take place.

The accuracy of accounts may also be questionable. There was plenty of scope for fraud, human error and faulty arithmetic, despite the audit, the Archdeacon's inspection and the annual turnover of officers. Such problems add to the fascination of parish accounts.

Churchwardens' Income
MEDIEVAL
Fund-raising was one of the major roles of medieval churchwardens. There was no uniformity in the way they raised their revenues. Donations, sales, rents, collections, fees and entertainment all yielded revenue, although many parishes relied on only one or two of these means. The methods used had implications for community life. A parish that depended on rents only needed an officer to collect them, whereas a parish that depended on church ales or collections required community involvement.

The nature of fund-raising in the medieval period depended to a considerable extent on Catholic doctrine: the dead souls in purgatory were aided by the prayers of the living; equally, the living were aided by the prayers of the saints in heaven. These doctrines had financial implications.

The veneration of saints could produce substantial sums if a church possessed their relics. Pilgrims to the shrine of St Urith at Chittlehampton (Devon) were donating an average of £50 per annum in the 1530s.[8] In 1370–71, the churchwardens of St Augustine, Hedon (Yorkshire) collected 6s 4d when its relics were carried around the town on the fair day of St Mary Magdalene. Living saints could also attract donations: anchorites were frequently held in high regard for their sanctity and received many offerings, which might be passed on to the church to which their cell was attached. In 1528–9, Allhallows, London Wall received 9s 3d 'of master Ankere of the gyft of dyuersse men and women of their dewocion at dyuerse tymys'.

The veneration of saints required the maintenance of lights before altars. Parish guilds raised substantial amounts of money for this purpose. Ashburton (Devon), Croscombe (Somerset) and Pilton (Somerset) all derived more than 10 per cent of their pre-Reformation income from guilds.[9]

Guild money-raising activities provided an important social function: their members expected to enjoy themselves. Their feasts and 'revels' were frowned upon by sixteenth-century reformers, despite the income raised. Not all of their income was used for 'lights'. Bodmin guilds vied with each other in raising money for the restoration of the church. The Prior of the Bristol Guild of Kalendars, after 1464, was expected to keep a library for the townsfolk.

The doctrine of purgatory was one of the most characteristic features of medieval religion. The faithful believed that the Pope had power to grant indulgences reducing the length of time the soul had to spend in purgatory. These indulgences were sold to raise funds. Their sale raised 16 pence for the churchwardens of Hythe (Kent) in 1412–13.

This was a relatively small sum and much more was raised from prayers for the dead, when their names were entered on bede rolls (see Chapter 5). Sometimes payment for entering a name formed a part of the clergy's emoluments. At Yeovil (Somerset), fees went to the churchwardens, amounting to 8 per cent of their income in the early sixteenth century.[10]

Other forms of commemoration also raised money. St Margaret's Westminster received many payments for funeral torches and tapers; its accounts effectively supply a mortuary register for the fifteenth century. At Stratton (Cornwall), churchwardens charged 4 pence for funeral knells to be rung in the early sixteenth century. Such entries are a particularly valuable source of information where parish registers of burials are missing.

The doctrine of purgatory and the veneration of saints resulted in many bequests for intercessory masses and lights before altars. The original motive for writing a will was religious, and testators were expected to remember the church when disposing of their possessions.[11] Wills are full of bequests to parish churches. These are sometimes recorded in accounts. Frequently, bequests were for intercessory masses, 'lights' before altars or payments to chantry clergy. Small sums were frequently given to the poor in return for their prayers. Wealthier testators could fund chantries for priests to say masses for their souls. 'Service' chantries funded such prayers for a specified term of years. Perpetual chantries provided for masses in perpetuity: they normally required the building of a chapel, or at least an altar, in the parish church, and the permanent employment of a priest. Sometimes, chantries were used for wider purposes: Dame Thomasina Percyvale's bequest in Week St Mary (Cornwall) required her chantry priest to conduct a school.

At Scarborough (Yorkshire), the chantry priest was expected to maintain an almshouse.

The fabric of churches could benefit substantially from bequests. In 1408 John Cable left £10 to the fabric of the nave at Frome (Somerset). The west tower at Wymondham (Norfolk) was paid for by fifty bequests. Many testators recognized that they had not paid tithes fully during their lifetimes: in 1518 Thomas Grey, priest, left 20 shillings 'to the high alter of St George's, Botolph's Lane, (London) for tithes forgotten'. He also left 20 shillings 'for the reparacions of the same churche'. Such payments may be recorded in churchwardens' accounts.

Legacies were frequently made in kind – cloths, brass pots, silver spoons, jewels – which were used to bedeck favourite images. At Wimborne (Dorset), no fewer than 130 rings, 3 silver spoons and 4 'great Buckylls of sylver and gilt' were hung on the apron of St Cuthberga. Such bequests might also be sold. In 1479, the wardens of Tintinhull (Somerset) received 5 shillings for a dress bequeathed by Peter Prettyll's wife.

Bequests of sheep and cattle were common. They could either be hired out or sold. At Elmsett (Suffolk) the 1543–4 accounts list thirteen cows bestowed upon the parish, together with the names of the donors, the purpose of the gift (they were all given to sustain lights before altars), and the names of the farmers. Even a city parish might have its own sheep: in the medieval period, a flock was owned by St Mary's, Bath. Bees were also kept. In 1528 William Potter left a hive of bees to the church at Morebath (Devon) to maintain lights before altars.

Wealthy benefactors sometimes gave land. In Halesowen (Worcestershire), a farm left to the church by Robert Pepwall brought in 8s 4d per year in the late fifteenth century. Many urban churches, such as St Michael's, Bath (Somerset) and St Michael's, Spurriergate, York, relied on rents as a major source of income. The churchwardens of Cratfield (Suffolk) were responsible for a variety of church property: the guild hall, the town house, the almshouse and the bakehouse.

Income could also be derived from pews. The earliest mention of pews in the historical record was in 1297, when the Statute of Exeter asserted the right of the bishop to allocate seats as he wished. It was enacted that 'no one from hence forth may claim a seat in church as his own, noble persons and patrons of churches excepted. He who for the cause of prayer shall first enter a church, let him select a place of prayer according to his will.'[12] Until the late medieval period, there was little or no seating in churches, except perhaps stone benches built into the wall. That is thought to be the origin of the epigram, 'the weakest to the wall'.

Pews became common in the fifteenth century. Churchwardens allocated seats to parishioners and drew up seating plans (discussed in Chapter 5). Technically, pew rents were illegal, although sometimes paid. Sale of seats was commoner. In 1457–8, the churchwardens of Yeovil (Somerset) received over 10 shillings from the sale of seats. In 1460–62, the churchwardens of St Margaret's, Westminster were paid fees ranging from 4 pence to 20 pence for the allotment of pews.

Many churches relied on 'gatherings' (that is, collections) among parishioners. At Cratfield (Suffolk), pre-Reformation accounts regularly record small sums raised by this means. Money 'gaderid' at St Michael's, Cornhill (London) totalled £3 19s 6d in 1456.

A collection was likely if major expenses had to be met. Much work was undertaken at St Andrew's, Holborn in the mid-fifteenth century. A sixteenth-century commentator noted that:

'all this, as many things else in the church in those days, even when the church had most lands, were nevertheless builded by money given of devotion of good people, then used to be gathered by the men and women of the parish in boxes, at ales, shootings, etc., for the only purpose through the parish weekly, during the time of these works as by their accounts, yet remaining, may and doth appear.'

In fifteenth-century Bodmin (Cornwall), the rebuilding of the church was attended with great enthusiasm: the rich gave trees from their estates; others gave stone, lime, timber and parcels of nails. The vicar gave his annual stipend; the poor gave their widow's mite or sometimes their labour. A total of £196 7s 4d in cash was raised between 1469 and 1472, but gifts in kind probably doubled that figure. This new Cornish church was symbolic of the great wave of church-building that took place in the fifteenth and early sixteenth centuries. Everyone pitched in to help.

Sometimes accounts of collections list donors; a great help to researchers. The account roll of St Laurence, Reading (Berkshire) for 1440–41 includes a list of eighty-six subscribers to the work then in progress; a total of £9 6s 5½d was raised.

Voluntary collections were occasionally replaced by compulsory rates, although these were not common before the Reformation. One of the earliest recorded rates was levied in 1367 to pay for the church spire at Bridgwater (Somerset).

Church ales provided a popular means of raising funds. Yatton (Somerset) rebuilt its nave, and added a tower and a porch, almost entirely on the proceeds of church ales. At Boxford (Suffolk), most churchwardens helped to organize ales in the year before they were elected, perhaps as a test of their abilities.[13] Ales were a popular means of socializing and of raising money at the same time. At Cratfield (Suffolk), they were the sole source of revenue in 1490 when they were held on Passion Sunday, at Whitsuntide and on All Saints Day; there were also two private 'ales'.

Many parishes had church houses where ales could be conducted and where the utensils used for brewing, baking and cooking could be stored. They were sometimes let out and their equipment could be hired; income from such arrangements is frequently recorded in accounts. The Tintinhull (Somerset) churchwardens depended heavily on the rent from their church house in the mid-fifteenth century. The church house at Stratton (Cornwall) was regularly used for church ales in the early sixteenth century. It was also let to merchants during fairs: in 1522, 20 pence was 'received of the Egyppcions for the church house'.

Dancing and plays were also popular means of fund-raising. At St Edmunds, Salisbury, 'alys plaies' – probably religious in character – raised money in the fifteenth century and 'dawnsyng mony' was regularly received at Whitsun throughout the sixteenth century. However, the dances were presumably repressed by the puritans in the early seventeenth century. Five

The church house at South Tawton (Devon).

Tintinhull (Somerset) parishioners staged a play in 1451 and gave the proceeds towards a new rood loft.

Sometimes plays could not have been staged without the cooperation of other parishes. In Oxford, the churchwardens of St Peter in the East kept a wardrobe of players' garments for hire. So did the churchwardens of Chelmsford (Essex), who received considerable sums from other parishes: in 1563 they received 53s 4d on two separate occasions 'for the here of our garments'.

Games of various kinds were used to raise money. At Croscombe (Somerset), the Robin Hood collection was conducted over two days by the youth guilds. On the first day, men captured women and demanded a forfeit; on the second day the procedure was reversed.[14] Such games turned the necessity of fund-raising into an entertainment which bound the community together. Conviviality was appreciated more than a mere tax levy.

Income could also be raised when fairs and markets were held. In Yeovil (Somerset), fifteenth-century churchwardens provided weights and measures, an anvil, and standings in their churchyard; in the sixteenth century they were loaning various pots and pans. Traders at St Bartholomew's Fair in early sixteenth-century London could hire standings on the property of St Botolph's, Aldersgate, although it is not clear whether this was in the churchyard itself.

POST-REFORMATION

The Reformation led to drastic changes in methods of fund-raising. The doctrinal underpinnings that had allowed parishes to raise money from indulgences, prayers for the dead and the veneration of saints disappeared. Relics ceased to be venerated, pilgrimages ceased, and the income of churches that had been their foci was decimated. Lights before altars went out, so the *raison d'être* for parish guilds disappeared. Sobriety was emphasized, so the drunkenness and debauchery thought to accompany church ales, plays and dancing led to their prohibition.

Fund-raising dependent on the doctrines of purgatory and the veneration of saints disappeared immediately. Ales, dancing, plays and games took longer to succumb. They were under puritan attack for a century after the Reformation. The Edwardian Commissioners, writing to the Bishop of Bath and Wells in 1547, thought that 'many inconveniences hath come by them' and required him to institute 'yerely collection for the reparacion of their churchies' instead.[15] However, church ales did have prominent defenders: in 1633 Bishop Pierce argued that 'by Church-ales heretofore many poor Parishes have cast their Bells, repaired their Towers, beautified their Churches, and raised stocks for the Poor.'[16]

51

The Boxford (Suffolk) churchwardens did not hold their regular church ale in 1547, the year when the arch-Protestant Edward VI came to the throne. At Mere (Wiltshire), ales were the major source of income until 1579 when a collection was made instead. An Act of Parliament in 1595 prohibited all 'church or parish ales ... may-games ... such unlawful assemblies ... mynstralysing of any sort, dauncyng, or other such wanton dallyeaunces' which led to 'disorders and contempts of law and other enormities ... increase of bastardy and of dissolute life'. No more was heard of the plays at Tewkesbury (Gloucestershire), which had been regularly held throughout Elizabeth's reign, after they were prohibited by the canons of 1603. By the eighteenth century, many church houses were either used to house the poor or were disused. Nevertheless, traditional practices continued in a few places: the 'clerk's ale' at Chiseldon (Wiltshire) was said to be still in existence as late as 1853.

Such changes reduced the finances of some parishes to dire straits. Morebath (Devon) staggered from crisis to crisis in the mid-sixteenth century. When lights before altars were extinguished, the vicar, Sir Christopher Trychay, bought the bees that had supported them. At Yatton (Somerset), income from communal drinking and feasting was down from over £13 in the early 1540s to just over £5 in Edward VI's reign. Income from gifts and bequests dropped to an all-time low: there was no point in giving to the church if the gift was then to be confiscated.

The impact of the Reformation on income was not, however, always negative. Everything depended on the way in which particular parishes were funded. Those that depended on rents were not significantly affected, unless those rents funded 'superstitious' purposes. Even then, it was possible to conceal such property from royal inquiries: the churchwardens of Cratfield (Suffolk) continued to draw rents from property that they should probably have surrendered throughout Elizabeth's reign.[17]

The activities of the iconoclasts brought in some revenue. At St Mary's, Holborn, 36s was received in 1547 for brass taken from tombs. At Cawston (Norfolk) over £44 was raised from the sale of church silver; most of it was spent on roofing an aisle, whitewashing the church and repairing the roads. Such sales may have formed a major portion of parochial income in the mid-sixteenth century. Many were prompted by the fact that the government was thought to be preparing to seize surplus parochial silver. Such fears were justified. In 1549, inventories of church goods were first ordered; other commissions followed and, in January 1553, the seizure of all plate and other valuables was ordered. These seizures have been described as 'an assault on the autonomy of the parishes of England'.[18]

Once churches had lost their pre-Reformation furnishings and their plate, the means for raising money were much more limited. Legacies could still be attracted, especially from puritans keen to promote the gospel by providing 'lecturers' in addition to the parochial clergy. In 1616, Ann Loyde left money to the churchwardens of Stratford on Avon. She instructed them to pay 6 shillings annually to 'a preacher to prech a sermon in the parish church yeirlie one the Sabboth day before St Thomas Day'. She gave money for church repairs, for the poor and for various other purposes. An extract from her will is entered in the Stratford on Avon (Warwickshire) vestry minutes. Testators elsewhere channelled legacies to the poor, to educational provision or to apprenticeships, through the churchwardens.

Despite the prohibition of prayers for the dead, deaths still cost money. Testators wanted a good funeral, whether their souls were going to purgatory or not, and wills sometimes included elaborate instructions for their conduct. A variety of fees could be incurred. The actual burial, the use of the parish bier and the ringing of bells; all had to be paid for. In 1553/4, the churchwardens of St Mary's, Reading (Berkshire) received 12 pence 'for the tolling of the bell' when Isabell Hopton died. Her executor, Edward Martyn, also paid 6s 8d 'for the grave', 12 pence 'for the paull', and a legacy of 20 shillings that she left to the church. At St Martin's, Leicester, fees for ringing the bells at funerals brought in over £4 in 1564–5 – a substantial proportion of that church's income. When such fees are recorded in accounts, they sometimes provide as much information as a burial register.

'Gatherings' could still be made, either in church or door-to-door. While parish ales were still permitted, many parishioners contributed in produce

The parish bier at Bampton (Devon).

– malt or wheat – that could be used to brew ale. The Minchinhampton (Gloucestershire) churchwardens continued to make their annual 'gatherings'until 1646, when a rate was substituted. Increasingly, voluntary collections morphed into compulsory rates.The voluntary element did not, however, die out. In the eighteenth and nineteenth centuries, when substantial sums were required, subscriptions were frequently solicited. A subscription funded church restoration at Stow (Lincolnshire), when the vestry refused to levy a church rate in 1848.

Rates had to be made with the consent of the majority of ratepayers. Apart from the incumbent (who was exempt), only those liable to pay had the right to vote. If no ratepayer attended the rate-setting meeting, the churchwardens themselves could make the rate. A rate could also be ordered by bishops and judges. Payment gave entitlement to claim a settlement in the parish (see Chapter 4), so assessors had to be careful not to assess those who might later claim poor relief. Rates could be levied by all the parish officers.

Church rates were of two kinds. Those for the repair of the church were levied on the occupants of land (whether they were parishioners or not), while those for the 'ornaments' of the church such as the bells, the pews and the clerk's wages were levied on parishioners' goods. Many rate lists survive in churchwardens' accounts or in separate rate books. The churchwardens of St Stephen's, Coleman Street (London) paid 34 shillings in 1608–09 'for making a book of all the householders names which have lands within this ward the better to levy aid'. In the seventeenth century, rates were usually levied either on the value of goods or the value of land. The latter was seen as both fairer and easier to assess.

Rate lists could serve a purpose wider than the merely fiscal. In Chester, and probably elsewhere, they were used as checklists of communicants, enabling non-attendees to be identified. They were also used to identify those who belonged to the parish and thus could be eligible for poor relief.[19]

Naturally, proposals to levy rates could meet with much debate and heavy resistance. Opposition to expenditure is a theme running through most vestry minutes and explains the constant interest in the Poor Law which will be discussed in Chapter 4.The Billericay (Essex) churchwardens in 1596 had not repaired their steeple because the vestry 'cannot agree whether it is to be repaired by every man's ability, or by every man's land, or by every man's devocion'. In 1817 the Kettering (Northamptonshire) vestry received a resolution from one of its committees to pay an assistant overseer a salary of not less than £80. They voted not to pay more than that sum. The incumbent of Cholesbury (Buckinghamshire) encouraged his vestry to levy a rate for church repairs in 1867 by agreeing, despite the fact that he was exempt from church rates, 'to pay his quota of rate as for a poor rate'.

Opposition was particularly virulent when rates funded unpopular expenditure. Archbishop Laud's demands for the beautification of churches caused many rates to increase in the 1630s. Between 1634 and 1638, the church at Prescot (Lancashire) was entirely re-flagged, many new pews were installed, the new altar was railed off, new bells were cast, an organ was installed and much other work undertaken. The township of Farnworth objected strongly to these improvements, which they had to help finance; it petitioned Parliament in 1640, asking to be made an independent parish. They particularly objected to excessive expenditure on the organ and on the organist's stipend. Others also objected: several gentry withheld payment of leyes and had to be sued by the churchwardens. The subsequent change of regime did not change Farnworth's attitudes towards the collection of Prescot's leyes; Parliamentary troops had to be used for the purpose in the mid-1640s.

The rating powers of the parish gradually disappeared in the nineteenth century as the functions of parish officers were transferred to other bodies. Church rates came to an end. Although it was illegal to fail to maintain a church, there was no legal sanction if a vestry refused to agree a rate. In the nineteenth century demands met with increasing opposition and refusals to pay, especially (but not solely) from nonconformists. Curiously, there was no statutory provision for levying them. They were authorized by custom, not by statute. It was not until 1868 – when they were abolished – that church rates were finally acknowledged in a statute.

Another source of income was provided by pews, as has already been seen. Their numbers increased after the Reformation; long sermons meant that parishioners needed seats. Pew rents were technically illegal until 1818 but at St Edmunds, Salisbury, receipts from them rose from 10s 6d in 1483–4 to £10 10s 8d in 1620. The late sixteenth-century churchwardens of Tewkesbury (Gloucestershire) had to levy heavy pew rents to make up for a lack of other income. Payment did not usually abrogate the right of churchwardens to change seating arrangements.

The Church Building Act of 1818 legalized pew rents.[20] Many of those who wanted a pew in the nineteenth century had to rent one. At St Michael & All Angels, Sydenham (Kent), pew rents in 1868 were fixed at prices ranging from £1 to 30 shillings per year. Churches could resort to pew renters for additional income. The vestry at Tunbridge Wells (Kent) resolved in 1898 that 'no Voluntary Church Rate be made but that in lieu of same, all seatholders in the Church be charged the usual 1/5th extra for church expenses'. Sometimes separate account books for recording the receipt of pew rents were kept, as at St James's, Trowbridge (Wiltshire).

Pew rents aroused much opposition. When the Incorporated Church Building Society began to make grants for building churches in 1818, it insisted on free sittings. Nevertheless, financial constraints meant that in many parishes pew rents continued to provide income well into the twentieth century.

In some places, pews were actually purchased or erected by pew-holders themselves. These were likely to become virtually a part of the freehold of particular properties, severely reducing the ability of the churchwardens to re-allocate pews in changing circumstances. A new gallery at Great Budworth (Cheshire) was delayed in 1798 because a pew stood in the way, and 'could not be conveyed for nearly two years yet to come as the Owner therof is a Minor'.

Churchwardens' Expenditure
FABRIC
The prime responsibility of the churchwarden was the fabric of the church. Apart from the chancel (the rector's responsibility), the building's future depended upon churchwardens. Virtually all accounts record fabric expenses. Payments to glaziers, plumbers, carpenters, masons and other tradesmen regularly occur, providing many glimpses of local networks of tradesmen and craftsmen, preserving their names from oblivion.[21] They may record successive generations of the same family engaged in the same occupation. For example, at Walton-on-the-Hill (Lancashire), the Corkers worked as glaziers and the Strange family as blacksmiths. It would be interesting to know what caused the ire of the Giggleswick (Yorkshire) vestry when they ordered

> 'that Robert Young and Richard Smith of Settle, Glaziers, shall for ever hereafter be discharged for doeing any work or being any further employ'd in any work hereafter to be done, in or about this church, for the gross abuses and ill usage the 24 believe the parish has sustained by the said Robert Young and Richard Smith.'

Tradesmen were not confined by parish boundaries, and the same names frequently recur in several neighbouring parishes. Sometimes the requirement for specialist skills, such as bell-founding, meant that craftsmen from distant cities had to be employed. The Croscombe (Somerset) churchwardens in 1506–07 employed masons from Exeter (70 miles distant) to build a new chapel, including an image of St George on horseback, at a cost of over £27.

Failure to keep the church in repair might cause serious problems. Churches literally stood or fell depending on the care given to them. A loose tile could easily be replaced. If it was not, several more could be ripped off by a storm; a few more storms might bring the roof down. However, the temptation to defer seemingly trivial works in order to keep the rates down was strong and many vestries fell into that trap. Churchwardens' presentments are full of complaints about broken windows and leaking roofs. In 1621, the churchwardens of Madehurst (Sussex) presented that 'There are some few stones fallen off from the church by tempestuous windy weather.' Such complaints were sometimes trivial, but the faults they reported on could lead to serious consequences. The vestry of St Edmunds, Salisbury was well aware that their church tower had become unsafe in 1651 but took no serious action to remedy the problem until it collapsed in 1653, taking with it most of the fabric of the nave. The churchwardens had the task of re-erection, and the cost was so great that rates had to be levied for ten years.

Accounts may enable us to trace in minute detail the work of repairs and renovations over many centuries. They also enable us to see how the church was looked after. In 1493, the churchwardens of St Andrew's, Canterbury paid 1d 'for caryyng away of ffylth of ye Chyrche'. At St Christopher Le Stocks (London), it was resolved in 1565 that 'yt is agreed yt the Glass windowe ou' the pticicon betwene the quyer & bodie of the churche to be mendid at the pishes cost'. There may even be mention of public toilets: the churchwardens of St Nicholas, Bristol recorded a payment made for repairing 'the pissinge place with-oute the churche Durre' in 1524.

Sometimes entries record extensive building work, as has already been seen in the case of fifteenth-century Bodmin (Cornwall). The Dunmow (Essex) accounts detail the money collected and, subsequently, 'layde out for the stepyll' in 1526. Weathercocks were cheaper: a new one at East Budleigh (Devon) cost 4s 1d in 1685. Innovations might also be recorded. In 1818 the vestry at St Giles, Cripplegate (London) ordered that gas 'be forthwith laid on in the Church, the expense of laying on not to exceed £100, and the expense not to exceed 16s. per annum for each burner'.

Internal furnishings were another churchwardens' responsibility. Before the Reformation, most churches had several altars and many images. At St Laurence, Reading (Berkshire), 6s 8d was 'payd to a Suffrygan for Halowyng of the High Awtr, Seynt Johns awtr, and a supaltare' in 1513. The rood (cross), with images of the Virgin Mary and St John at its foot, was usually hung above the archway between the chancel and the nave. Side chapels frequently served as chantries where mass could be said on behalf of its founder(s) to reduce their time in purgatory. Painted images of patron saints

A modern restoration of the rood, with Saints Mary and John, at Bruton (Somerset).

were usual. The rood screen and loft were common objects of expenditure: in Hedon (Yorkshire), their erection in 1379/80 was the chief call on churchwardens' coffers. Wall paintings of biblical scenes were also common. In 1467, the churchwardens of Yatton (Somerset) spent £4 'to peynt our Lady'.

New work on church fabric continued even during the dissolution of the monasteries. The churchwardens of Halesowen (Worcestershire) acquired a rood, an organ, images and pictures from its dissolved abbey. A stained-glass window from Barlinch Priory (Somerset) was installed in Morebath church as late as 1538; its priest, Sir Christopher Trychay, simply did not comprehend the destruction that was about to ensue.

THE REFORMATION

That destruction, and the attempted restoration in Mary's reign, is recorded in detail in churchwardens' accounts. Innumerable altars, images, wall paintings and stained-glass windows were lost. The altar at St Laurence, Reading (Berkshire) was sold in 1548, replaced when Mary came to the throne in 1553, and removed again after Elizabeth's accession. It was replaced by a communion table in 1568, when 22d was paid 'To Martyn Woodnett for makinge of the Frame for the communion table'. Another 4 shillings was paid 'To the joynor for making the comunion table and benches, with a doore'.

A few rood screens do survive, although most fell victim to the sixteenth- and seventeenth-century iconoclasts. The Mere (Dorset) churchwardens paid 12 pence 'for the defacynge of the Images of the xij Apostles whiche were paynted in the face of the Rode lofte' in 1559–61. The transept at Hedon is now 'much mutilated and defaced', and the same fate presumably befell the screen mentioned above. Sometimes a lot of work was involved in removing structures no longer needed for the conduct of the reformed liturgy. The accounts for St Mary's, Reading (Berkshire) recording the money 'payede for the taking downe of the Quyer in the Abbye' after the Dissolution occupy twenty-one pages of the printed edition. At North Elmham in 1541, the churchwardens needed stones for work on their own church and spent 16 pence on 'a lode of fre stone' from the ruins of Walsingham Abbey.

It was much easier to get rid of the wall paintings of biblical and mythical scenes that adorned most churches. All that was required was a bucket of whitewash, frequently mentioned in accounts. Some paintings were replaced by the Lord's Prayer and the Ten Commandments: the written word, only accessible to those who could read, superseded the pictures which everyone could understand. Did the replacement reflect the fact of increasing literacy? Which came first: the text, or the literacy?

Window glass was difficult to replace. William Harrison, writing in 1586, described how 'stories in glasse windows' still remained in many churches. Much painted glass survived until the civil war. In 1644 the churchwardens of Lowick (Northamptonshire) paid 12 shillings for 'glasing the windows when the Crucifixis and scandalus pictures was taken downe'.

Medieval religion was perhaps at its most vibrant on the eve of the Reformation. Historians struggle to explain how such popular practices as pilgrimages, lights and masses for the dead were swept away. It is astonishing that there was not more resistance. Nevertheless, resistance there was. Accounts record expenditure but frequently do not distinguish between duty, enthusiasm and opposition. They can, however, be inadvertently revealing. At Stratton (Cornwall), the churchwardens took down the rood on the orders of the Edwardian regime but the accounts show that it was immediately reinstated when the Prayer Book Rebellion broke out in 1549. At Morebath (Devon) accounts record that many vestments were hidden from the Edwardian commissioners and brought out for use again when Mary came to the throne. Similar concealment was going on all over England; churchwardens and clergy engaged in what has been described as a 'panic-stricken stampede to prevent theft by the crown'.[22] The return of Roman Catholicism under Mary was greeted with enthusiasm. Churchwardens spent much on replacing what had been lost: for example, the rood reappeared in almost every church. At St Andrew Hubbard, Eastcheap (London), the restoration of Catholicism was both expensive and rapid. Most parishes spent more on fabric than loyalty required, and continued to embellish their churches until the moment of Queen Mary's death. By the end of 1554, most high altars had been replaced. However, there was a limit to what churchwardens could afford. The government showed little interest in restoring the veneration of saints. Consequently, images of saints were rarely re-erected (apart from images of Mary and John beneath the rood, required by an order of 1556); their altars were mostly unrestored; lights were not burnt before them.

When Elizabeth reintroduced Protestantism, there was much less enthusiasm and the cost caused many churchwardens to hesitate. It took decades for some of them to fully comply with her orders. At St Kew (Cornwall), it was not until 1576 that the removal of the rood was even discussed. The rood loft, altar and images at Masham (Yorkshire) were not burned until 1571. Numerous parishes were presented for their failure to destroy images during the Northern visitation of 1567.[23] As late as 1585, Tewkesbury (Gloucestershire) still retained vestments that had no Protestant use.

Disused steps to rood lofts can still be seen in many churches, as in this example at Bruton (Somerset).

The arms of Elizabeth I in Beckington Church (Somerset).

Altars, images, roods and painted glass were replaced by commandment boards and the royal arms. The boards were 'to be read not only for edification, but also to give some comlye ornament and demonstration that the same is a place of religion and prayer.'[24] Setting up the royal arms was presumably intended to show that the church was a place of loyalty to the Crown. In 1565, the churchwardens of Strood (Kent) paid 14s 4d for 'paynting and wrytynge ye Armes and rood loft'. Perhaps they hoped that by placing the royal arms on the rood loft, they would not have to take it down again.

During the Interregnum, many royal arms were taken down. In 1649–50, East Budleigh (Devon) spent 6 pence on this task. However, joy at the return of Charles II led many to re-erect them. The Prescot (Lancashire) churchwardens acted as soon as they heard the news of the Restoration. New royal arms cost St Columb Major (Cornwall) no less than £18. Post-Restoration erection of the royal arms demonstrated spontaneous acceptance of the restored regime; they were not required by statute or canon law. Quite what they said about the holiness that Archbishop Laud had once hoped to find in a church building is another question. Nicholas Harpsfield, the Marian Archdeacon of Canterbury, had no doubt: he called the royal arms set up in place of the rood the 'abomination of desolation standing in the temple that Daniell speaketh of'.[25]

Laud's concern for the beauty of holiness resulted in many parishes restoring their altars and railing them in during the 1630s. For Laud, the altar was 'the greatest place of God's residence on earth, greater than the pulpit'. It therefore had to be a decent permanent structure at the east end, railed in, and not the mere table in the nave preferred by puritans. Churchwardens' compliance with Laud's orders is recorded in their accounts; the extent of their enthusiasm is not, although visitation records may throw some light on puritan resistance.

Yet more reversals of policy and doctrine followed the Restoration in 1660. When the bishop visited St Edmunds, Salisbury (Wiltshire), he ordered that the seats at the east end (where the altar had previously stood) should be removed and replaced by the 'comunion table with rails there decently placed'. He also ordered the reinstatement of the font. Poor churchwardens!

WORSHIP

Throughout the Reformation, worship was the *raison d'être* of the church. All the controversy centred on how it should be conducted. Costs, however, were incurred, whatever liturgy was used.

Before the Reformation, much money was spent on wax for the provision of 'lights' before images and altars. They symbolized the 'light of Christ'. A tenth-century canon required a light to be burning before the altar during mass. This idea was gradually developed: thirteenth-century canons required a light to be burning at all times; by the fourteenth century the candles were on the altar rather than around it. The proliferation of altars meant the proliferation of candles. Churchwardens provided them, although, as we have seen, parochial guilds and bequests in wills yielded much of the funding. Wax for candles consumed almost a third of churchwardens' early sixteenth-century expenditure at Masham (Yorkshire) during the latter years of Henry VIII's reign. Such expenditure ended with the Reformation.

The conduct of worship was a matter for the incumbent rather than the vestry. However, vestries did concern themselves with worship. Before the Reformation, the accounts of Allhallows, London Wall, record many names of additional clergy; mainly chantry priests and guild chaplains. Special services had to be paid for. When Henry VIII died in 1547, Worcester's St Michael in Bedwardine had to pay 'at the Kynge's highnes dirige and masse'. Five tapers cost 10 pence; the ringers were paid 6 pence and supplied with ale costing 4 pence; a further 4 pence had to be spent on 'two papers of the Kyng's Armes to sett on the Kyng's horse'.

Until the Reformation, the priest provided the bread and wine used at mass. The medieval laity generally only partook of the bread and then only once a year. Instead, on most Sundays they were given bread blessed by the priest to eat after the service. This 'holy bread' was supplied by churchwardens, who frequently organized collections to pay for it. At Bolney (Sussex), accounts include a list of forty-eight parishioners expected to contribute to the cost.

After the Reformation, more frequent communions, and the fact that communicants received both bread and wine, meant that costs soared. Since the elements were now consumed by the laity, their provision increasingly became the responsibility of churchwardens. At Repton (Derbyshire), Easter communion bread and wine was paid for by the priest in the late sixteenth century but the churchwardens paid costs for other communion services. Collections to pay for the pre-Reformation 'holy bread' were replaced by collections to pay for communion bread and wine. The rubric of the second Edwardian prayer book specified that the elements were to be provided by the curate and churchwardens jointly. In 1601–02, the Kilmington (Devon) churchwardens asked 'Allowance for bread & wyne for the Comunion this yere' costing 10s 6d. The canons of 1604 specified that bread and wine were to be provided by the churchwardens.

The frequency with which the ritual was conducted is reflected in the purchase of bread and wine in the accounts. At Shillington (Bedfordshire), purchases were made twice a month in 1579. When a new vicar was instituted in 1592, the frequency dropped to three or four times a year. The Shillington accounts also tell us that both malmsey and claret were used. The more expensive wine was reserved for the more 'respectable', hierarchy being reflected even in the wine that was drunk at communion.

Cost was sometimes an issue. That may be one reason why communion services were somewhat neglected at Pittington (Co. Durham) in the early years of Elizabeth's reign. No payments for bread and wine were recorded prior to Bishop Barnes' 1587 visitation. Immediately after the visitation, 'a botell to bring home the wyne in', and disbursements for the elements, were entered in the accounts. Had the bishop ordered the neglect to be rectified?

Some puritans opposed celebrating communion at Christmas and Easter, while high churchmen encouraged it. During the Interregnum, the parishioners of Walton-on-the-Hill (Lancashire) had to be examined to see whether they were 'worthy' to receive communion; failure to purchase bread and wine may indicate that clergy feared this would exclude too many of their parishioners and therefore did not celebrate communion. After the Restoration, and until the mid-twentieth century, many parishes celebrated communion no more than three times a year: at Christmas, Easter and Whitsun, the minimum required by canon law. The accounts of Brentor (Devon) for 1737 record payment for bread and wine only at these festivals.

Communion was not the only service that cost money. The routine services of priests had to be paid for. Before the Reformation, casual priests brought in to say masses for the dead, or to read bede rolls, sometimes appear in churchwardens' accounts. Sometimes, the reading of the bede roll was regarded as an additional duty for the parish priest. In 1489–90, the churchwardens of St Mary at Hill (London) paid 8 pence 'To Mr John Redy for rehersing of the bederoll'. Redy was the parish priest.

Following the Reformation, the emphasis on preaching meant that sermons were in great demand. The Interregnum churchwardens' accounts of St Giles Cripplegate (London) are full of payments for sermons: for

The Jacobean pulpit at Monkton Farleigh (Wiltshire).

example, in 1654–5 shillings was paid to 'Mr Kelly for a sermon on a thanksgiving day for the peace concluded between England and the Netherlands'. Half a century later, the aged Bishop of Gloucester was also the vicar of this church. A vestry minute of 1706 records 'The Bishop requesting this Vestry to choose a Lecturer for this Parish and recommending for their choice Mr Thomas Sawyer, they debated the same for some time and then dispersed themselves without coming to any resolution thereon.' The emphasis on preaching meant that the pulpit was used more than it had been before the Reformation. In the remote parish of Hartland (Devon), 33s 4d was 'pd for a new pulpit' in 1609–10. Hour-glasses also had their uses. At Prestbury (Cheshire) in 1672, £1 7s was paid 'for the Houre Glasse, Houre Glasse Case, and the guildinge and the setting upp the same'.

VESTMENTS

Priests conducting services needed to be properly vested. Before the Reformation, that could mean heavy expenditure. A suit of vestments bought for Bassingbourn (Cambridgeshire) cost as much as £24. The parishioners of Morebath (Devon) spent many years raising money for a fine new set of black vestments for the celebration of requiem masses. The process can be traced in detail through the accounts. Sadly, just after the vestments were finally purchased, a new set of injunctions led to the order that black vestments could no longer be used. Simplicity became the order of the day, with many puritans objecting even to a surplice. The absence of references to the washing of a surplice in the accounts of Northill (Bedfordshire) between 1581 and 1604 tends to confirm that Anthony Hoggett, who was deprived of his curacy in 1604 for his puritanism, did not wear one. A new surplice was bought in 1604, and payment for washing it resumed.

The Edwardian inventories of church goods (see Chapter 5) record many vestments surplus to what the Commissioners thought necessary. The churchwardens of St Dionis Backchurch (London) compiled an extensive list of the vestments they sold in 1550. However, the black Geneva gown became popular, and royal support for a distinctive clergy dress ensured that vestments continued to be used, except by some clergy such as Hoggett.

SERVICE AND OTHER BOOKS

Churches required books containing orders of services and readings. Before the Reformation, the text of the divine office was contained in the breviary. The manual provided the texts used for administering the sacraments, the processional contained the words of the litany used in processions (hence the name), and the antiphonary contained the text of sacred chants. In 1507, Pilton (Somerset) had 'a masse book printed', 'iiij prosessionaries prynted', 'a manel boke prynted', and 'a grete purtuas of prynte'.

These books were rendered redundant by the Reformation and were sold off or destroyed. At St Botolph Aldersgate, the churchwardens reported that 'the people understood not' when Latin service books were sold. Such sales were very unpopular, and the churchwardens were very careful to record that they had been made with the assent of the whole parish, or at least of the vestry, so that they could not be held personally responsible. Service books had to be replaced during Mary's brief reign. The Boxford (Suffolk) churchwardens over-spent on these items in the early years of Mary's reign.

The Reformation brought with it many new books, all of which had to be supplied by the churchwardens. Henry VIII required every church to have an English bible; under Edward VI, two successive prayer books were ordered to be used. Queen Mary reverted to the old services, but another new prayer book was introduced when Elizabeth ascended the throne. Other books were also required. Edward VI expected churches to have the *Paraphrases* of Erasmus. The injunctions issued by Queen Elizabeth in 1559 required clergy to read one of the homilies 'set forth for the same purpose by the Queen's authority' every Sunday. They also required every parish to provide 'one book of the whole Bible of the largest volume in English', together with the *Paraphrases* of Erasmus. The need for new books continued into the seventeenth century with the introduction of the King James bible, the (temporary) substitution of *A Directory for the Publique Worship of God* for the *Book of Common Prayer* during the Interregnum, and the latter's reintroduction in a revised form in 1662, still used in some churches. Churchwardens had to find the money to pay for all these. Such payments are recorded in their accounts.

At Mildenhall (Suffolk), the early Edwardian churchwardens purchased Erasmus's *Paraphrases* for 5s 4d, using the money received for their old service books. Other new books soon followed: the *Book of Common Prayer*, a bible and four psalters. The purchase of a Geneva bible in 1585 indicated the puritanism of the parish. Halesowen (Worcestershire) churchwardens bought a bible as soon as Cromwell issued his injunctions in 1537, and were equally quick off the mark with subsequent injunctions to purchase new titles.

Not all churchwardens were equally obedient. When the first Edwardian prayer book was issued in 1549, the churchwardens of Sampford Courtenay (Devon) acquired a copy. Their priest used it for the first time on Whit Sunday. His congregation promptly rose in rebellion, together with many others in Devon and Cornwall. They were defeated, but did not have long to wait before the old religion returned under Mary, and the old liturgy was restored.

When the prayer book was reintroduced by Elizabeth, the churchwardens of Yatton (Somerset) paid 5 shillings 'for the boke of common prayer'. The churchwardens of St Nicholas, Warwick, however, were slow to obey the Elizabethan injunctions; it was not until 1562–3 that they paid 5 shillings 'For the Boockes of the Homilies'. Copies of the *Paraphrases* and the *Homilies* were purchased for Sheffield (Yorkshire) parish church in 1564. During the Northern Rising of 1569, many churchwardens helped to reinstate Catholic rituals and burnt such books. When the authorized version of the bible appeared in 1611, it was three years before the churchwardens of St Mary's, Devizes (Wiltshire) paid £2 5s to 'Saml Clark for a new Bible of the new Translation'. Churchwardens were even slower to obtain copies of the *Directory* that replaced the *Book of Common Prayer* in January 1645. By the following June, only 10 per cent of parishes had done so. There was a much more enthusiastic response to the reintroduction of the *Book of Common Prayer* in 1660.

MUSIC

Music was popular. In the sixteenth and seventeenth centuries, it was generally provided by organs. However, they were expensive, and many rural parishes did not acquire one until the nineteenth century. Several were commissioned by the early sixteenth-century churchwardens of St Michael Spurriergate, York. The 'organ pllayur' at Wigtoft (Lincolnshire) received 7s 7½d in 1580. The organ project at Prescot (Lancashire), mentioned above, had been closely supervised by the bishop himself: the churchwardens visited Great Lever Hall, his Lancashire residence, to discuss the matter on several occasions.

Music was not, however, always favoured by puritans. In 1562, a vote in the Lower House of Convocation avoided a proscription of organs by one vote. The use of the organ at Northill (Bedfordshire) was discontinued in 1583 and it was sold in 1590. Some parishes remembered how royal commissioners had seized church goods under Edward VI, and made appropriate provision: at St Laurence, Reading (Berkshire), the organ was sold in 1578 to prevent it being 'forfeited into the hands of the organ-takers'. Such fears had justification. In 1644 an order for the destruction of organs was made by the Long Parliament, and some were destroyed. The Prescot (Lancashire) vestry anticipated the order: with no bishop to exercise authority over them, their organist was dismissed in 1642 and their new organ sold a few years later.

Churchwardens' accounts reveal the presence of few instruments other than the organ in the sixteenth and seventeenth centuries. In the eighteenth and nineteenth centuries, however, church bands became common in country parishes, using instruments such as the bassoon, violin, flute and hautboy. Payments for such instruments are common in accounts of the late eighteenth century. At Youlgrave (Derbyshire), 19 shillings was paid 'for one Haughtboy and Reeds' in 1790. Barrel organs became popular at the end of the eighteenth century, despite their limited repertoire.

Congregational singing was uncommon in the sixteenth century. The *Book of Common Prayer* did, however, make provision for music, and the psalms were increasingly sung. Four song books of Genevan Psalms were purchased for Sheffield (Yorkshire) parish church in 1570. Its organ was repaired four times between 1560 and 1572, even though the psalms were usually sung unaccompanied. The work of men such as Richard Baxter, Isaac Watts, and especially the Wesley brothers, popularized hymn-singing in the eighteenth century, when the purchase of hymn books begins to be recorded. A singing gallery was erected at Ugborough (Devon) in 1775. In the nineteenth century, choral music became popular following the success of Walter Hook's choir at Leeds (Yorkshire). Numerous choir stalls were installed throughout the country, filling up the space in chancels that had been left vacant by the sixteenth-century reformers. They can still be seen.

Sometimes music was provided by travelling musicians. It is not clear whether the 3s 4d paid 'to minstrels for playing and singing in the church' at Barnstaple (Devon) in 1552–3 was for music to accompany worship or for more secular entertainment.

FONTS

Fonts, used for baptism, did not attract much attention during the Reformation and were rarely replaced before the seventeenth century. Ancient fonts tended to be retained when other church furniture was replaced. However, Laudian concern to enhance the font's dignity attracted puritanical ire in the 1630s. Consequently, the Long Parliament forbade their use: baptism was to be administered from a mere basin. The font at Prescot (Lancashire) was taken down well before the order to do so arrived. At St Martin's, Leicester, 5 shillings was spent on 'a bason to be used at baptism' in 1645, but in 1661 it was 'agreed that the font of stone formerly belonging to the church shall be set up in the ancient place, and the other now standing near the desk be taken down'.

BELLS

Church bells attracted little attention from the puritans, although in Devon

The early sixteenth-century bell-tower at Evesham Abbey (Worcestershire).

Steeple Ashton (Wiltshire) church tower. It lost its steeple in the seventeenth century when struck by lightning.

and Cornwall they were temporarily silenced after the 1549 rebellion, as they had been used to support the rebels. They had a variety of uses in addition to funerals; expenditure on bell ropes and other equipment suggests that they were rung far more frequently than is the case today. Baldricks (the leather strap suspending the clapper), bell ropes and other equipment frequently appear in accounts. Sometimes the bells themselves required attention. Shillington (Bedfordshire) had bells recast in 1575, 1579, 1588 and 1602–03.

Bells were regularly rung before services. In North Devon they were rung when a fox was known to be in the vicinity; everyone joined in the fox hunt.[26] They were rung to welcome distinguished visitors and to announce official jubilation. The bells of Northill (Bedfordshire) were rung in 1565 as Queen Elizabeth passed by. An Act of Parliament required bells to be rung to celebrate the foiling of the gunpowder plot. Thundery weather was another occasion on which bells might be rung, as the chimes were thought to ward off lightning. One wonders how many church towers were struck by lightning while ringing was in progress!

THE CLOCK

By the fifteenth century, many churches had clocks. The new clock at St Mary's, Reading, in 1611/12 cost £40, and subscribers' names are listed in the accounts. At Prescot (Lancashire), a new clockhouse was built after the visitation of 1633. Despite its association with more controversial work on the fabric and the sale of the new organ in 1643, it attracted no opposition and was allowed to remain under the Long Parliament and Commonwealth. Clocks were inoffensive to both puritans and high church

The church clock at Steeple Ashton (Wiltshire).

The sundial above the porch at North Bradley (Wiltshire).

These chimes were installed at St Giles, Cripplegate (London).

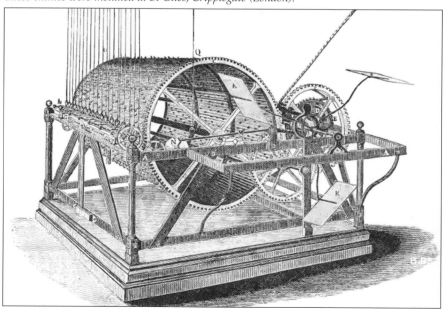

men; indeed, they performed a function from which all could benefit, and did not attract iconoclasts. In this period most people did not have watches, so relied on the church clock for the time. A cheaper alternative was a sundial, as can be seen at North Bradley (Wiltshire).

ADMINISTRATION

Churchwardens were seen as representatives of their parish in both ecclesiastical and secular courts. They provided both themselves and others with sustenance when they went about the parish's business. They had to attend visitations, make presentments and pay the appropriate fees. They also had increasing secular responsibilities under the Tudors and Stuarts. The cost of dealing with royal, civic and ecclesiastical dignitaries took 1 per cent of London churchwardens' budgets c.1470, and 5 per cent under James I.[27]

The presentments of churchwardens were important. They could lead to punishment, which might involve expenditure. Offenders against canon law could be censured by the church courts and ordered to do public penance. They had to stand dressed in a sheet, carrying a white wand, to confess their faults to the entire congregation. At Otterton (Devon) the churchwardens paid a shilling in 1714 to 'procure sheet and wand for Peter Longworth standing penance'. The better-off frequently avoided such penalties by paying a fine. The poor could only avoid it by suffering excommunication.

If a church had to be re-consecrated, that too required expenditure. The church of Great St Mary, Cambridge was the burial place of Martin Bucer, the famous protestant reformer. His funeral in 1551 evidently attracted great crowds, so much so that the churchwardens had to spend 2 pence to repair seats afterwards. That did not go down well with the Marian ecclesiastical authorities. In 1557, the churchwardens had to spend 8 pence 'For the new halloweinge or Reconcyleing of our chyrche for beyng interdicted for the buryall of Mr bucer, and the charge thereto belongeing frankensens and swate perfumes for the sacrement and herbes etc.'

Routine episcopal supervision cost money. Attendance at visitations could be expensive, especially when overnight accommodation was needed. Archbishop Laud's visitation in 1634 cost Littleham (Devon) over 13 shillings. On such visitations the church hierarchy had to be wined and dined: in 1625 the churchwardens of All Saints, Derby paid 6s 8d 'for a bottle of Clarett wyne and qtr of sugar to Mr Archdeacon'.

Churchwardens themselves tended to view food and drink as one of their perquisites. In 1560, the newly-elected churchwarden of St Alphege, London Wall recorded 'pd the fyrstt Day that I was chusyd wardyn for our breakfast at the tavern' 4s 2d. Any occasion was thought to provide a good opportunity to eat together at the parish's expense: 'for our breakefast that Day that we Dyd serch abought the p'sshe for pyctures and images that were paynted', 3s 4d.

Sometimes the cost of such entertainment was questioned. The cost of a parish dinner at Grappenhall (Cheshire) was struck out by magistrates in 1768. The parishioners had their revenge by refusing to attend meetings when the 1771 and 1772 surveyors' accounts were presented. Parishioners enjoyed parish feasts. At Selsey (Sussex) it was the churchwarden himself who was presented 'for that he made no provision of dyet for the poore that went about the bounds of the parish in the perambulation'. Beating the bounds of the parish was hard work, needing refreshment!

The provision of food and drink was routine. So was cleaning the church. Before churches were paved, rushes were regularly strewn on the floor, both for cleanliness and for warmth. Churches had to look their best for important visitors. At St Martin in the Fields (Middlesex), 12 pence was spent 'for Rishes and strawing herbes when the bishoppe came in visitacion to ye churche'. Paving, of course, would be much preferred to rushes. The churchwardens of St Petrock's, Exeter paid 5s 2d for stone 'que vocatur pavyngstone' in 1464/5. In many country parishes, earth floors did not disappear for another couple of hundred years. The vestry of Houghton le Spring (Co. Durham) ordered that 'a cess of iiid in the pound shalbe levied for winninge of flaggs' in 1604.

During periods of unrest, churches might be used as prisons. That fate befell the church of Walton-on-the-Hill (Lancashire) when it was occupied by 700 captured royalist soldiers after the Battle of Worcester in 1651. They were confined for a month. The churchwardens had a substantial bill for cleaning up the resultant filth, whitewashing the walls and repairing the damage.

The account book itself had to be paid for. The Hartland (Devon) churchwardens paid 3 shillings 'for this accompte Booke bought att Exon' by John Abbatt and 'by hym brought home for nothinge'. He had a long journey – the distance by modern roads between Hartland and Exeter is almost 72 miles – and the account book is rather large! The accounts themselves had to be written up at the end of each year of office, so that there could be a straightforward handover of responsibility to the new wardens. The churchwardens of St Edmund's, Salisbury paid a scribe 3s 4d to do this in 1495; by 1632, they were spending 6s 8d on the same task. Inflation is not a new problem.

It was not only the accounts that had to be written up. Bishops' transcripts of the parish register and other official returns had to be prepared. Routinely, the churchwardens had to make their presentments at visitations. In Manchester there were so many to be written in 1666 that 5 shillings had to be paid for a scribe. Inventories of church goods had to be written when, in 1550, the Edwardian government decided to confiscate church goods. The churchwardens of St Mary's, Cambridge paid 'for wryghtynge the invytory of our church goodes & Jewelles to delyuer to the Kynges Maiestes commysyners'. Inventories of church goods are discussed in Chapter 5.

LIBRARIES

In a few parishes, small parochial libraries were formed. At Tilney All Saints (Norfolk) 2s 6d was paid out in 1479 'to ye booke byndar for ye chenyng of ye bokus in ye library & for ye amending of ye bokys in ye qwyer'. Books were valuable, so were chained for protection. The Repton (Derbyshire) churchwardens' accounts include a 1622 list of 'Bookes sent by Mr Willm Bladone to be employed for the use of the parrishe'. They include works by Bishop Babington, Mr Perkins and Mr Dod, among others. They also include 'towe books of Martters'; that is, John Foxe's work. This was probably Derbyshire's first lending library and its lending rules were written in the account book.

Many parochial libraries, primarily for the use of the clergy, were founded as a result of the initiative of Dr Thomas Bray in the early eighteenth century. Expenditure on them is sometimes recorded in churchwardens' accounts.

SOCIAL ACTIVITIES

Both vestries and churchwardens concerned themselves with social activities. Church ales and plays have already been discussed. A 'King's Revel' was regularly held at Croscombe (Somerset) in the sixteenth century; however, there had evidently been some difficulty in persuading people to take the role of 'Lord' of the feast, so much so that the vestry felt compulsion was necessary. They ordered 'that all suche yonge men as shall hereafter by order of the hole parryshe be chosen for to be lorde at Whytsontyde for the behafe of the churche, and refuse so to be, shall forfeyte and pay for the use of the churche iiis iiijd.' The following year Harry Keen was chosen and refused to act, so paid the fine.

Social events involved expenditure, although they might also raise funds. The bonfire at Westminster on St Margaret's Eve in 1495 required an expenditure of 3 pence for faggots plus 'rewards' for singers from the King's Chapel. Officers of both the King's palace and of Westminster Abbey, who arranged the loan of hangings, also had to be rewarded. The bonfire was probably the reason why two night watchmen had to be paid by the churchwardens on that night.

SECULAR RESPONSIBILITIES

Churchwardens gained a wide variety of secular responsibilities under the Tudors, which also had to be paid for. Little was spent on secular matters before the mid-sixteenth century. Thereafter, increasing responsibilities meant increasing expenditure. Poor relief (see Chapter 4) was frequently a prime concern, at least until 1834. Churchwardens worked closely with other parish officers to relieve the poor, maintain the parish armour and its plough, and pay county rates to support the maintenance of bridges, hospitals, the county gaol and maimed soldiers.

The eradication of vermin was another churchwardens' responsibility. A statute of 1533 ordered every parish to keep a crow net. The failure of the Leominster (Shropshire) churchwardens to do so led to their presentment in 1566. No fewer than three Acts were passed under Queen Elizabeth to deal with vermin, and small boys could earn good money by trapping them. In 1624–5, the Hartland (Devon) churchwardens paid 2d to 'John Beares sonne for a fitchewes head'. A fitchew was a polecat. Dead foxes were worth more: Degory Cholwill and John Buse both received 12d for foxes' heads in the same year. Considerable amounts were sometimes paid. In East Budleigh (Devon), the cost in 1804 amounted to more than a quarter of the churchwardens' income.

New responsibilities were acquired under the Lighting and Watching Act of 1833. This was permissive: it enabled vestries to pay for watchmen, street lighting and the maintenance of fire-fighting equipment. The Kettering (Northamptonshire) vestry voted £110 in 1834 to have the town lit by gas. The following year they voted £45 to employ watchmen, increased again to £60 in 1836 to include the cost of maintaining fire engines. In 1848 they had an engine-house built. A small minority steadily opposed expenditure on such projects.

It was not only legislation that gave churchwardens responsibilities. They also had responsibilities towards their local community. The churchwardens of Prescot (Lancashire), for example, found themselves travelling in search of corn during the famine years of 1648–50.

Highway Surveyors' Accounts

Highway surveyors' expenditure was frequently included in churchwardens' accounts, and separate surveyors' accounts are only occasionally found. Parishioners frequently thought there was little need for expenditure: statute labour, fines on defaulters, payments for exemption, and perhaps a highway ale sufficed to keep the highways repaired to local satisfaction, but not necessarily to the satisfaction of travellers. Highway rates could be imposed under legislation of 1691 at the initiative of surveyors; yet surveyors were reluctant to take the initiative. Quarter Sessions could, however, fine parishes that failed to maintain their roads adequately. The fine (paid by a rate) would be used to carry out the required repairs. This method of proceeding was frequently used as it absolved the surveyor from the unpleasant responsibility of imposing a rate on his neighbours.[28]

The work of the surveyor is reflected in vestry minutes and accounts. In 1747, the Wimbledon (Surrey) vestry ordered 'Mr Haines to do his statute or pay to the highways for a ploughland'. In 1769, they also ordered that 'the men kept in the workhouse by the parish are to work on the roads and nowhere else'; they were to be given 'such encouragement' as the highway surveyors thought proper.

The use of pauper labour on the roads was common but not always successful. If paupers received no additional payment for the work, they were likely to do as little as possible. The vestry of Wheatley (Oxfordshire) insisted that paupers should be paid 'at a fair price by the yard' for their work, although they also insisted that they should pay for any damage to the tools used from their wages.

Other parishioners were expected to bring their own tools, although at Grappenhall (Cheshire) the parish provided some: in 1735 a new marl pick had to be provided at the cost of 3 shillings, as the old one had been stolen. Most of the work consisted of filling up potholes.

Expenditure was occasionally required. The Wimbledon vestry authorized the expenditure of up to £20 for repairing the road 'from the corner of the wall of Mr Banks's across the Green to the Crooked Bilett' in 1759. In 1785, the Grappenhall surveyors paid 2 shillings to 'Jas Robinson for surveying and mapping' land acquired for a road.

The 1797 accounts of Joseph Collington, 'overseer' of the highways of Seagrave (Leicestershire), include many names of the men he employed on roadworks. On 11 June 1797, he paid Michael Smith £1 for ten days' work, Thomas Glover 6 shillings for three days' work, William Benskin 3 shillings for two days' work and himself 6 shillings. In the following year, Richard Benskin took over as overseer and levied a rate of 6 pence in the pound. His assessment lists all the ratepayers in the parish for 1798.[29] The accounts of surveyors, once allowed by the Justices of the Peace, should have been given into the safe custody of churchwardens or overseers, with a duplicate copy made for the use of succeeding surveyors.

Constables' Accounts

Constables' expenses, like those of surveyors, are frequently recorded in churchwardens' accounts. Occasionally, however, separate accounts survive. Their accounts were audited, and not always found to be satisfactory. When the inhabitants of Hathersedge (Derbyshire) checked the accounts of their constable, Rowland Swanne, in 1665 they found them 'to bee very Fowle unworthy debouched wastfull and expensive soe that wee Utterly dislike and disapprove of the same'.

The constable's prime responsibility was for law and order and for dealing with malefactors; he also looked after the village lock-up, cucking stool, stocks and other local means of punishment. At Buckland in the Moor (Devon), John Bull was paid 10 shillings 'for a pair of stocks' in 1654. These required 'Iron worke' costing a further 6 shillings and a further 9 pence was spent on 'bringing home of the said Stocks, from Aisberton'. In 1598 the constable of St Michael, Cornhill (London) paid 13s 2d 'For making of Irons

The lock-up at Steeple Ashton (Wiltshire) was the responsibility of the parish constable.

So were these stocks at Kenton (Devon).

to the pillory for a whipping place, for locks, paynting and to the Carpenter in all'.

Constables had to ensure that offenders were escorted to appear before the Justices and that punishments ordered were carried out, although they did not necessarily carry them out in person. At Melton Mowbray (Leicestershire), Robert Moodee was paid 2d 'for wippin tow pore folkes' in 1602. They were presumably whipped for unlicensed begging, then given 2 pence and sent to their parish of settlement, where they were entitled to claim poor relief.

In Manchester, 2 shillings was paid 'for a cart when John wyrall was carted' and a further 16d for 'one to drive it and for their whippinge'. The offender was whipped 'at the cart's tail': that is, he was tied to the back of a cart and whipped as the cart was driven. Imprisonment also incurred costs: the Kilmington (Devon) accounts for 1567–8 show 2 shillings paid to 'fraunces banke and Thomas Crandon for watche and warde wh a pprysoner i day and i nyght'.

Before punishment, offenders had to be caught. Constables raised the hue and cry when an offence had been committed and paid for precepts when they came from other parishes. The constables of Manchester regularly paid 8 pence for such precepts. A typical example from their accounts reads: 'Item paid for making precepts for Hue and crye which came from wackffield the xxjth of februarye 1618 [1619] after one Edward Choster who had stollen certen goods from Rychard Scoffield.'

Whipping a beggar.

Constables took their orders from Justices of the Peace; they were also subordinate to the high constable of the Hundred. They were required to make presentments at Quarter Sessions of offences committed within their jurisdiction, but frequently reported ,'omnes bene' (all well). When William Newsome of Glossop made his presentment to the Derbyshire justices in

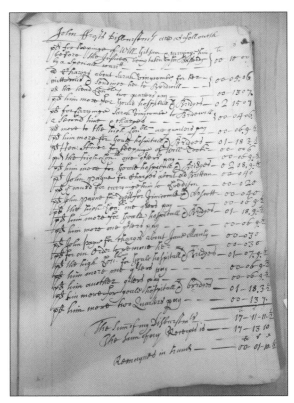

A page from the constable's accounts of Shobrooke (Devon).

Transcript of the Shobrooke (Devon) Constable's Accounts

John Frosts disburstmts are as followeth

Pd for keeping of Will Gitssam & carrying him before the Justices being taken up for bastardy by a special warrtt:	00-10-00
Pd charges about Sarah Vinycombe for her mittemis & sending her to Bridwill	00-05-06
Pd the head Conble two quarters pay	00-13-07
Pd him more for Goale hospital & Bridges	02-15-07
Pd for Carryinge Sarah Vinycombe to Bridewell a second time & charges	00-04-06
Pd more to the high Conble one quarters pay	00-06-9½
Pd him more for Goale hospitall & bridges	00-18-3½
Pd Hen Hines for keeping of Will Tooke	00-00-6
Pd the high Conble one qters pay	00-16-9½
Pd him more for Goale hspitall & Bridges	02-08-9½
pd John Payne for Charges about old Brittan	00-04-0
pd ye guard for carrying him to Crediton	00-02-0
pd John Payne for dyett for Vinicombe & Arscott	00-04-0
pd the high Constble one qrters pay	00-06-9½
pd him more for Goale hospitall & Bridges	01-18-9½
pd him more one qrters pay	00-06-9½
pd John Payne for charges about Jane Manly	00-03-0
pd for an order to remoue her	00-03-0
pd the high conble for Goale hospital & Bridges	01-07-9½
pd him more one qrters pay	00-06-9½
pd him another qrters pay	00-06-9½
pd him more for goale & hospital & bridges	01-18-3½
pd him more two Quarters pay	00-13-7
The sum of my Disbursmts	17-11-11½
The sum of my Receipts is	17-13-10
Remaynes in hand	00-01-10½

1689, he was more specific: 'I have no popeish recusants nor grayhoundes nor quakers nor guns to ye best of my knowledge within my liberty.' Even so, he was expected to be present at Sessions. The Wimeswold (Leicestershire) constable recorded in 1635 that 2s 6d was 'spent when I was before the Justices at Syston to presente the Recusantes and the punishing of Roagues'. The summoning of juries was another responsibility of the constables. At Repton (Derbyshire), the constable's accounts recorded 6 pence 'spent in warning a jury for the Crowners [coroners'] quest'.

Constables had responsibility for some economic functions. Every parish had its own weights and measures which had to be checked against the King's standard, usually kept at the county town. The constables of Repton had to take theirs to Derby, where it cost them 12 pence 'payd for ye town weaghtes and measures to ye Clarke of ye market'. They also paid sixpence 'to ye Clarke of ye market for a p'clamation'.

Constables collected and paid county rates to the high constable of the Hundred every quarter. There were originally separate rates for maimed soldiers, gaols, hospitals, bridges and Poor Law administration. In 1738, the County Rates Act lumped these all together in a single county rate.

In addition, constables also collected national taxes. Their accounts rarely record receipts; their expenses, however, were recorded since these had to be recovered locally. In 1636, the Wimeswold constable recorded 3s 4d spent on 'makinge the Billes the last yeare and this yeare which the inhabitantes was severally taxed and assessed to pay towardes the making of his Maties Shippes'. During the civil war, constables were expected to collect 'contributions' imposed by local garrisons. Stathern (Leicestershire) accounts list regular supplies of provisions to the Royalist garrison at Belvoir Castle in the early 1640s. Constables continued to be responsible for levying taxation into the eighteenth century. In 1790, the Hooton Pagnell (Yorkshire) constables paid over £1 'for land tax instructions'.

Purveyance was another imposition met by constables. This levy was imposed to meet the cost of royal progresses. At Cratfield (Suffolk), 26 shillings was 'payed unto the Constabells for the Quens gesse' during Elizabeth's visit to the county in 1572. The constable of Woodbury (Devon) purchased a bullock in 1575 'for the quenes maiestye'. When Charles I travelled to Scotland in 1641, the constable of Upton (Nottinghamshire) had to provide him with horses. Purveyance was abolished after the Restoration.

One of the major responsibilities of the constable was to ensure that the parish played its role in the defence of the country; indeed, the very name 'constable' was military in origin. In 1466, an Act of Parliament directed that every Englishman should have a longbow of his own height and that butts should be set up in every parish. This legislation remained in force for several centuries, enforced by the constables. At Eltham (Kent) 12 pence was paid in 1603 'for felling three trees for the buts and cutting them out'. There was further expenditure for carriage, for nails, for labour and setting the butts up and – as always – 'in charges for their suppers for all them that wraght at the buts'.

Every parish had its armour, usually stored in the church tower but regularly brought out for musters. Armour had to be paid for by levying a rate. In Hartland (Devon), £5 8s 9d was collected from 'a rate made for the buying of Armor for the Churche, and to be imploied in other affaires for her mates service' during 1597. Armour and weapons had to be repaired: Roger Syncocke was paid a penny 'for mending the head of one of the Churche pikes' and an unnamed tradesman was paid 'for a Hilt a handle and a Scabert for a sworde & for mending of a Dagger of the Churche'.

High constables regularly checked up on the state of parish armour and sometimes required an inventory to be made. A St Martin's in the Field (Middlesex) inventory of 1598 records

'iij Arming swords, one horsemans sworde and ij backe swords , vj Salevers and a horsemans peece, iiij flaskes and touche boxes, iij Daggers, iiij white Corsettes and ij blacke Corslettes, iij Almayne Ryvettes, iiij morrions, iiij Salettes, one buffe Jerkyn, one Coate of Mayle, ij blacke bills and vi Pykes.'

The Pittington (Co. Durham) vestry took action itself in 1622, ordering 'that upon Easter Teuese day yearly in the fore noone the whole six common armors shalbe brought in and viewed be the twelve of the parish, what case it is in, that it may be mantaned and keept as it ought to be.'

When the importance of gunpowder began to become evident in the sixteenth century, constables sometimes purchased considerable amounts. They could levy a rate for the purpose: at St Columb Major (Cornwall), a rate for purchasing gunpowder made in 1596 brought in £7 3s 9d. The church housed 74lb of gunpowder stored in barrels, plus 9lb of old powder. This use of the tower could be dangerous: in 1676, mischievous boys set off an explosion at St Columb and severely damaged the church.

Defence in an age without modern communications required a means of conveying messages rapidly. That was provided by the construction of beacons at strategic points. The constables had responsibility for building and watching them. At Stratton (Cornwall), 8 pence was paid in 1544 'for making the bekyn at launcells'.

Rebellion in Tudor England was an ever-present possibility. The accounts of North Elmham (Norfolk) provide evidence of the 1549 rising. Arrows, swords, daggers and scabbards were purchased, the butts were repaired and the beacon was watched. The sum of 5 shillings was spent 'towarde ye setting forthe of ye Soudyours of northelmhm & other'. Herry Ruston, one of the churchwardens, recorded 'the sumes of monye payed & delyued by me … in ye tyme of ye Campe at Mussolde wt ye Assent & consent of the ynhabytance of ye Townchype of Elmhm'.

He paid for food and drink, for 'hys Cart & Horses to Cary wt vytalls to the seyd Campe' and for a variety of other things. This expenditure was almost certainly not for the support of the Crown. A further 12 shillings was 'delyued to those of ye Townchype of Elmhm yt went ffyrst to ye Campe at Mussholde, that ys to seye, to xij of them'. The inhabitants of North Elmham are shown to have been rebels from the evidence of their churchwardens' accounts. The same applies to their contemporaries in Morebath (Devon), as has already been seen.

In the seventeenth century the threat of rebellion had not disappeared, and constables were expected to be on their guard. The Walton on the Hill (Lancashire) constable presumably accompanied the high constable when he went 'thrugh the parish in Disarming and taking notise of all the armor weapons and Furniture belonging to recusantes' in 1641.

Perhaps more important than the armour were the soldiers. All able-bodied men aged from 16 to 60 were obliged to undertake military service. Constables had to ensure that they appeared at musters. Sometimes they drew up muster rolls listing all their men (although these rarely appear among parish records). Soldiers had to be paid: the Whitchurch (Devon) churchwardens paid 6s 6d to 'the muster master pay for thirteen sholders' in 1687. The constables of Manchester paid 2 shillings to John Ffyshe in 1613 'for beatinge the drum ii days at the generall Muster'. The arming of the Restoration militia takes up much space in the constables' accounts of Upton (Nottinghamshire) for 1660–61. When men had to be pressed for actual military service, the task of doing so fell to the constable.

It was also the responsibility of the constable to ensure that edicts of Crown and Parliament were implemented. In 1641–2 they, together with the minister and other parish officers, had to take the Protestation oath before a Justice of the Peace and then had to ensure that it was administered to their parishioners. The accounts of St Clement, Ipswich (Suffolk) reveal what happened next: £3 12s was paid 'For wryghting faire of 700 names of them that took the protestation to deliver to Mr Bailies'. Very occasionally, lists of those who took oaths such as the Protestation or the 1643 'Solemn League and Covenant' were preserved in parish chests. For example, at

Fire hooks in the church at Bere Regis (Devon).

Steyning (Sussex) the churchwardens' accounts include the names of those who took the Covenant, and at Pentrich (Derbyshire) Protestation signatures are in the parish register. Many returns to the 1641–2 Protestation oath are now in the Parliamentary Archives.[30]

In time of plague, the role of the constable was particularly important, as he was responsible for quarantining sufferers. At St Christopher le Stocks (London), 6d was spent on 'red wandes and bylles for the plague' in 1573, and in 1625 6s 8d was spent on 'setting up the Crosses on the visited houses'. During the plague outbreak of 1652–3, the constables of Prescot (Lancashire) hired Lawrence Croft for dangerous work: he was to 'fumigate houses, bury infected corpses, and guard quarantined plague contacts in special wooden cabins on the outskirts of the town'.

Constables were also responsible for fire precautions. Leather buckets, ladders and strong iron hooks for pulling down burning thatch were frequently stored under church towers. In Northampton, the church books reveal that there were 190 buckets in the four churches of that town in 1628. At St Martins in the Field (Middlesex), 18 pence was 'Paide unto vj poore men for helping home with the hoockes and lathers from Durham house when the stable was a fier'.

Guild Accounts

Before the Reformation, accounts were sometimes kept by the wardens of parish guilds.[31] The wardens of altars at Walsall (Staffordshire) also had their separate accounts. Guild accounts rarely survive, although those of the stewards of the

Fraternity of Jesus Mass at St Edmund's, Salisbury, have been published,[32] as has the register of the Fraternity of the Holy Trinity at St Botolph, London.[33] The latter includes not just fifteenth-century accounts but also lists of members, rules, a calendar of deeds and other miscellaneous memoranda.

Further Reading
A more detailed discussion of churchwardens' accounts, specifically aimed at family historians, is given by:
- Brown, Mike. *Guide to Churchwardens' Accounts: A Practical Guide for Family Historians.* (Dartmoor Press, 1997, available on CD).

The classic account of churchwardens' accounts is:
- Cox, J. Charles. *Churchwardens' Accounts from the Fourteenth Century to the Close of the Seventeenth Century.* (Methuen & Co., 1913).

The accuracy and value of churchwardens' accounts is debated in:
- Burgess, Clive. 'Pre-Reformation Churchwardens' Accounts and Parish Government: Lessons from London and Bristol', *English Historical Review* 117, 2002, pp.306–32.
- Kümin, Beat A. 'Late Medieval Churchwardens' Accounts and Parish Government: Looking beyond London and Bristol', *English Historical Review* 119, 2004, pp.87–99.
- Burgess, Clive. 'The Broader Church? A Rejoinder to "Looking beyond"', *English Historical Review* 119, 2004, pp.100–16.

Churchwardens' accounts have been extensively used by Reformation historians. On this, see:
- Hutton, Ronald. 'The Local Impact of the Tudor Reformation', in Haigh, Christopher, ed. *The English Reformation Revised.* (Cambridge University Press, 1987), pp.114–38.

There are numerous printed editions of parish officers' accounts, vestry minutes, etc. Churchwardens' accounts published before 1939 are listed in:
- Blair, Lawrence. *A List of Churchwardens' Accounts.* (Edwards Brothers, 1939).

Many older editions are available online, as noted in Chapter 2. Printed editions cannot all be recorded here but some very useful introductions are included in:
DEVON
- Hanham, Alison, ed. *Churchwardens' Accounts of Ashburton, 1479–1580.* (Devon & Cornwall Record Society, new series, v. 15, 1970).
GLOUCESTERSHIRE & BRISTOL
- Burgess, Clive, ed. *The Pre-Reformation Records of All Saints' Church, Bristol.* 2 vols. (Bristol Record Society, 46 & 53, 1995–2000).

LANCASHIRE

- Steel, Thomas, ed. *Prescot Churchwardens' Accounts 1635–1663.* (Record Society for Lancashire and Cheshire, 137, 2002).
- Ramsay, Esther M.E. & Maddock, Alison J., eds. *The Churchwardens' Accounts of Walton-on-the-Hill, Lancashire 1627–1667.* (Record Society of Lancashire and Cheshire, 141, 2005).

LONDON

- Burgess, Clive, ed. *The Church Records of St Andrew Hubbard Eastcheap c.1350–c1570.* (London Record Society, 34, 1999).

For full listings of London churchwardens' accounts and vestry minutes with notes on their contents and associated documents see:

- *Churchwardens' Accounts of Parishes within the City of London: A Handlist.* 2nd ed. (Guildhall Library, 1960).
- *Vestry Minutes of Parishes within the City of London ... .* 2nd ed. (Guildhall Library, 1969).

NOTTINGHAMSHIRE

- White, Edward, ed. *Village Government and Taxation in Later Stuart Nottinghamshire: The Gedling Town Book 1665–1714.* (Thoroton Society of Nottinghamshire, 45, 2010).
- Bennett, Martyn, ed. *A Nottinghamshire Village in War and Peace: The Accounts of the Constables of Upton, 1640–1666.* (Thoroton Society Record Series 39, 1995).

OXFORDSHIRE

- Price, F.T. *The Wigginton Constables' Book.* (Phillimore, 1972).

SUFFOLK

- Middleton-Stewart, Judith, ed. *Records of the Churchwardens of Mildenhall: Collections (1446–1454) and Accounts (1503–1553).* (Suffolk Records Society 54, 2011).

SURREY

- Drew, Charles, ed. *Lambeth Churchwardens' Accounts 1504–1645, and Vestry Book 1610.* 2 vols (Surrey Record Society, 18 & 20, 1941–1950. Also available on fiche as East Surrey Family History Society Record Publication M82 [199-?]).
- Cowe, F.M., ed. *Wimbledon Vestry Minutes 1736, 1743–1788.* (Surrey Record Society 25, 1964).

WILTSHIRE

- Swayne, Henry James Fowle, ed. *Churchwardens' Accounts of S. Edmund & S. Thomas, Sarum, 1443–1702, with other documents.* (Wiltshire Record Society, 1896).

Chapter 4

THE POOR LAW

The church has always considered it a duty to give alms.[1] The bible is full of exhortations to support the poor. That was a major part of the justification for collecting tithes (see Chapter 7). Before the Dissolution, the duty was frequently discharged by monastic houses which received a high proportion of tithe income. It has been estimated that monasteries alone paid out £6,500 per year in alms before 1537.[2] Paupers also benefited substantially in other ways: chantries, fraternities and obits usually made provision for them in return for their prayers. They were frequently mentioned in wills. William Townsend, vicar of Ugley (Essex), instructed his churchwardens to distribute 3 shillings 'yerly at the day of my obite' when he died in 1514.[3] Originally, the word 'pauper' meant poor. In the eighteenth and nineteenth centuries a much more pejorative sense of the word came into use: a pauper became someone claiming poor relief.

The poor were rarely mentioned in medieval churchwardens' accounts. The parish, as an institution, had very limited involvement in poor relief. Parishioners expected to support poor kin, mentioned the poor in their wills, and may have given other private assistance. However, they also paid tithes, which they expected the clergy to use in part for poor relief.

Charitable provision changed dramatically in the mid-sixteenth century. The dissolution of the monasteries ended a major source of institutional support. The granting of indulgences for charitable purposes also ended. The only remaining institutions capable of meeting the needs of the poor were the parish and, in towns, the municipal corporation. The latter frequently worked with the parish. After 1660 some nonconformists, especially the Baptists and the Quakers, looked after their own poor, but their numbers were tiny.

After the Dissolution, poverty steadily increased and the government realized that something had to be done. Its approach was governed primarily by a concern for public order rather than charitable considerations. The demographic causes underlying the growing numbers of poor were not understood. The population was growing and children unable to earn their own living formed an increasing percentage of the population. In some areas, too, the onset of enclosure resulted in mass unemployment. Leicestershire, for example, was badly affected.[4]

The earliest legislation was an Act of 1531, significantly entitled 'How aged Poor and Impotent Persons compelled to live by alms shall be ordered.' It authorized Justices of the Peace to licence beggars. Subsequently, parishes were authorized (in 1546) to make charitable collections and to set up poor boxes (in 1547). The 1604 canons required churchwardens to provide 'a strong chest with a hole in the upper part thereof' to be positioned 'in the most convenient place, to the intent the parishioners may put into it their alms for their poor neighbours'.

Originally, such boxes were much used. At St Albans (Hertfordshire), the 'lockes of the poore mans boxe' had to be mended in 1594. In the 1620s and 1630s, the poor box at St Botolph without Aldgate (London) regularly yielded between £20 and £30. However, by the end of the century its use had diminished. Eighteenth-century poor boxes had little use. When the one at Daventry (Northamptonshire) was opened in 1786, for the first time in seven years, it yielded the paltry sum of 3s 9½d. Just over a year later, the curate found the even paltrier sum of 5 farthings.

The Tudors recognized that poor boxes were insufficient. The particularly serious problems posed by London's poor were tackled in 1547 by the levying of the first compulsory poor rate.[5] In 1563, Parliament required 'two able persons' in each parish to be 'gatherers and collectors of the charitable alms'; 'when the people are at the church at divine service' they were to be 'gently' asked 'that they of their charity will be contented to give weekly towards the relief of the poor'.

The results of such legislation were variable. At Ludlow (Shropshire), the published sixteenth-century accounts record no expenditure on the poor. The poor were absent from the churchwardens' accounts of Ashburton (Devon) until weekly pay was instituted in 1543–4. By 1600, however, much was being spent on the relief of the poor, orphans and the sick. In 1595, the parish officers of Stratton (Cornwall) reported to the Justices the names of ten orphans 'wholly relieved' by the parish and claimed that over 100 paupers received regular relief.

The prime motivation for the Poor Law was the perception of the gentry that increasing numbers of wandering beggars posed a threat to society. According to the preamble to the 1662 Act of Settlement,

'poor people are not restrained from going from one parish to another, and therefore do endeavour to settle themselves in those parishes where there is the best stock, the largest commons or wastes to build cottages, and the most woods for them to burn and destroy;

and when they have consumed it, then to another parish; and at last become rogues and vagabonds; to the great discouragement of parishes to provide stock, where it is liable to be devoured by strangers.'

Vagrants aroused much suspicion: in a sample of 1,604 vagrants' examinations drawn from various counties between 1561 and 1641, 45 per cent were suspected of theft, although there was no proof in half of these cases.[6]

A proactive approach was taken by Parliament in 1536, when parishes were ordered to provide work for vagrants, to make weekly collections for the impotent and to punish beggars. Harsher measures, prescribing branding and enslavement as punishments for vagabonds, were taken in 1547. This was soon repealed, but paupers were required to wear badges from 1555, and compulsory poor rates were introduced in 1563. More comprehensive legislation was passed in 1572: beggars were to be whipped, Justices of the Peace were to register the names of the 'aged, decayed and impotent poor', collectors of assessments and overseers of the poor were to be appointed, monthly 'views and searches' of the poor were to be undertaken, and licences for beggars were authorized. This established a system for the following quarter-century, until harvest failure in 1596 and 1597 prompted the legislature to take another look. The Elizabethan Poor Law Acts of 1598 and 1601 provided for the appointment of overseers who would relieve the impotent, bind out pauper children as apprentices, set paupers to work and levy poor rates when necessary. Begging was forbidden, except by licence, and vagabonds were to be whipped by constables. There were subsequently a few minor tweaks but in their essentials these Acts provided the basis for poor relief until they were replaced by the Poor Law Act of 1834.

The parish and its overseers did not entirely lose their Poor Law role in 1834. Over 80 per cent of relief continued to be given by overseers as out-relief, rather than in the new workhouses.[7] Overseers continued to collect the poor rate until they were themselves abolished in 1925, although after 1865 the rate was determined by the number of paupers settled in the union rather than in the parish. The system was finally abolished in 1948.

The 1598 legislation placed responsibility for the relief of the poor squarely upon the parish. There was no reliance on voluntary contributions. Nevertheless, grandparents, parents and children were required to support each other. Some grandparents were compelled to take in their grandchildren, and adult offspring were compelled to support their parents. There was a network of kin solidarity through which informal support was provided.[8] Provision by the parish was only made if kin were unable to cope. The poor could also glean in the fields at harvest-time, they might have rights of common enabling them to keep a cow or pig and to gather fuel. Neighbours frequently provided for them. Parish support was not always necessary and might be additional to other support. As Robert Doughty put it in 1664, a weekly allowance to a poor family should amount only to 'what with their work will maintain them'.[9]

Under the Elizabethan legislation, at least two overseers were to be appointed for each parish. Churchwardens held the office *ex officio*. Overseers could levy poor rates and had to relieve every pauper who could claim 'settlement' in their parish. The concept of 'settlement' was to be a bugbear of the migrant poor for several centuries, although they quickly learned the rules and knew how to manipulate them to their own advantage. They knew where they wanted to be legally 'settled', and JPs frequently relied entirely on paupers' recollections to determine settlement. It was easy to manipulate or withhold relevant information. For example, Joseph Polyblank had held the office of Plymouth town crier for some years. However, he wanted to claim settlement in West Alvington (Devon). Since office-holding conferred settlement, he claimed that the town-criership had been served by deputy and that he had not been paid. The overseers accepted his settlement on the basis that he had rented property in West Alvington, and decided that a formal examination before a Justice was unnecessary.

Parishes were only responsible for paupers 'settled' within their boundaries, so the poor could only be relieved by their parish of settlement. If they claimed relief elsewhere, they could be removed by a Justice. Even if they did not claim relief, they could still be removed: all that was necessary to initiate removal, before 1795, was to be deemed likely to become a burden on the rates. That applied even when children were supporting their parents, despite the fact that they were required to do so under the 1601 Act. Such parents could still be ordered out of the parish if it was not their parish of settlement. Overseers were just as likely to prevent the fulfilment of family obligations as to insist upon them.[10] If they wished to remove newcomers to the parish, they had forty days in which to complain of their presence to a Justice. After 1795, removal could only take place if the person concerned actually claimed relief.

Not everyone who could have been removed actually was. Removal was expensive: until 1814, paupers had to be escorted if they were removed to their place of settlement. Overseers frequently preferred to leave well alone. Furthermore, the 1662 Act (see below) only applied to those who came to a parish in order to 'inhabit' there. It did not apply to many migrants and other travellers who were just passing through. They might be the responsibility of parish constables under the vagrancy laws.

Settlement was strictly defined by the 1662 Act of Settlement and subsequent legislation. Those deemed to be settled in a particular parish were:

- those born in the parish where their parents had legal settlement, even (and importantly) illegitimate babies
- those who had paid rates on property in the parish[11]
- serving or former apprentices (provided the master had a settlement)
- serving and former parish officers
- anyone in service in the parish for one year or more
- anyone settled in the parish for more than forty days, provided that they gave public notice of their intention to settle.

A married woman took her husband's settlement; children aged 7 and under took their parents. If overseers regularly paid relief, that was taken as recognition of the pauper's right to settlement in that parish. If settlement could not be determined (as in the case of abandoned children), then the pauper was regarded as having a settlement wherever they happened to be when claiming relief.

Overseers were particularly keen to ensure that any pregnant unmarried woman was removed from their parish before she gave birth, otherwise the cost of poor relief for the child would fall on them. Forcible removal of such women was banned in 1732. However, from 1743 an illegitimate child took its settlement from its mother, not its birthplace.

Transients faced serious obstacles if they wanted to settle, as parishes wanted to reduce the numbers who could claim settlement. Masters could be persuaded to offer their servants contracts of less than one year, so that they were unable to gain a settlement. Vestries could question the settlement of particular individuals. In 1783, the Gnosall (Staffordshire) vestry required twelve persons whose settlements were regarded as suspect to be examined by a magistrate. 'Such as are likely to be troublesome' were to be removed. Many vestries followed the example of Pittington (Co. Durham) whose 'twelve' ordered in 1622 that

'no inhabitant within the parish … shall receive, harbour and entertaine any stranger to be his tenant or tenants into his house or houses before he acquaint the twelve with his entent, and shall himself and two sufficient men with him enter in bond with him to the overseers that neither his tenant, wife, or children, shall be chargeable to the parish for five years next following upon paine and penalty to forfeit ten shillings for every moneth.'

Such bonds may survive among parish records.

There were many disputes between parishes concerning the settlement of individual paupers. Parishes to which paupers were sent frequently objected and, indeed, threatened retaliation. A note on a settlement certificate sent from Minchinhampton (Gloucestershire) to Bisley in 1789 reads:

'Gentlemen. As we understand you are going to remove such of our parishioners as reside in your parish home, we therefore think it necessary to hint to you that we have numbers of familys of yours residing with us which will afford us an ample field for example.'

The settlement laws were not affected by the Poor Law Act of 1834. However, it was becoming increasingly difficult for the poor to alter their legal settlement. Traditionally, farm servants had been hired by the year, thus allowing them to gain a settlement. Such hiring was in sharp decline in the early nineteenth century, so the primary means for young men to gain a settlement was ceasing to be available. This was remedied by the Poor Removal Act of 1846, which made anyone who had resided continuously in a parish for more than five years irremovable. The period was reduced to three years in 1861 and one year in 1865. The concepts of settlement and irremovability were distinct in law but, after 1876, three years' residence in one place without claiming relief conferred settlement.

Disputes concerning settlement were decided by Justices of the Peace. Quarter Sessions spent much of their time deciding appeals against removal orders. Quarter and Petty Sessions records should therefore be consulted by researchers interested in Poor Law issues. Pilbeam and Nelson's edition of mid-Sussex Poor Law records makes a detailed comparison between parish Poor Law documents and Quarter Sessions records. Much settlement business was conducted in Petty Sessions, and their minute books enable us to trace the activities of parish officers as they went about their business.

The Poor Laws placed great restraint upon the free movement of the poor, although the Act did permit labourers 'to go into any county, parish or place to work in time of harvest, or at any time to work at any other work' if they had a certificate from the minister or one of the officers of their parish. In practice, most of those removed were men with families, and women. Young, unattached males were seldom removed, as their labour was needed. Overseers' strictness in implementing the law varied. It was up to them to judge who was 'likely to be chargeable' and they used their discretion. It is likely that they were stricter in the late eighteenth and early nineteenth centuries, when the demand for relief soared.

Sometimes census-type listings of the poor were drawn up in order to get an overall view of local needs. *An ease for overseers of the poore* published in 1601 suggested that such lists should, for each household, include the names and ages of the occupants, their state of health, their usual employment, their weekly earnings, the name of their employer, those unemployed, those fit for apprenticeship, those who boarded orphans and others, weekly allowances and a note of those licensed to beg. In 1614, the vestry of North Nibley (Gloucestershire) ordered the constables to take a census of strangers, cottagers and inmates. Such documentation helped overseers determine eligibility for relief and surviving lists are invaluable to researchers.

Despite the restraints placed upon them, the pre-1834 Poor Laws gave the poor a sense of entitlement to poor relief in their parish of settlement. Having a settlement could mean the difference between starvation and survival. Consequently, the right to a settlement was highly valued and closely guarded. Claimants frequently possessed detailed knowledge of settlement law and sought to arrange their affairs so that they could claim relief in a parish which offered generous relief. They were also prepared to riot if adequate relief was not forthcoming.[12] The processes of claiming relief are mostly hidden from historical reconstruction. Unless magistrates were involved or letters survive, a pauper's interaction with overseers is rarely revealed in the sources until his claim was admitted and relief paid.

Despite attempts to make paupers work, overseers found that the easiest way to provide relief to the poor was to pay a dole. These were of two kinds: regular and casual. Widows, the aged and the impotent were likely to receive a regular weekly payment, perhaps reassessed yearly. The unemployed and those whose wages needed supplementing received casual payments determined by overseers (although subject to Justices' supervision). Such payments were never universal.

Accounts frequently record the names of recipients and the amounts paid, although not necessarily why payments varied. The Gnosall (Staffordshire) overseers allowed Robert Mosse 6 pence per week in 1682 but gave Mary Taylor only 5 pence and Margaret Davies 4 pence. In 1751, weekly allowances varied between 6 pence and a shilling.

Sometimes, paupers 'settled' in one parish but resident elsewhere could be given relief. In 1777, Anne Caudwell 'living in Stafford Town' received over £2 from Gnosall. Such arrangements avoided the cost of removal and could, in certain circumstances, help paupers to gain a settlement in a different parish.

Despite the harshness of the law and of many parish officers, kindness could still be shown: in 1800, the Gnosall overseers allowed Matt Tunniclift one penny 'for tobacco'. However, in 1826 they also recorded that 'William Owen wants everything. Allowed nothing.'

The Poor Laws created a vast pile of documents. One of them, the licence to beg, was authorized by various sixteenth-century statutes including those of 1552 and 1563; it was retained in the Poor Law Act of 1598 but dropped in the consolidation of 1603. The licence authorized deserving poor to beg in a given area, usually only within their parish or their Hundred. It was retained by the beggar and consequently copies are rarely found. Their issue was not recorded.

The vagrant's passport was also retained by the vagrant but may be recorded in accounts and other documents. Those who acquired these passports were, by definition, convicted of the crime of vagrancy and were undergoing punishment. They were likely to be whipped: the Honiton (Devon) churchwardens paid John Clatworthy 2 shillings in 1643 'for caning vagerents'. They were then given relief, together with a passport allowing them to return to their parish of settlement and to claim relief along the way. Passports should have been signed by the constables in all the parishes through which they had to pass. Payments to such vagrants were frequently recorded in accounts, although sometimes their names are not given. In 1632, for example, the Cratfield (Suffolk) constables paid 6 pence for '2 poor vagrants taken in the town for their relief, their pass making, whipping, and conveying unto the next constable'. The passports themselves rarely survive, apart from a few collected by parish officers at the receiving end. Puddletown (Dorset) overseers kept them with the relevant settlement examinations (discussed below). Many paupers probably failed to reach their destination, especially when they had long distances to travel. Also many passports were forged: between 1740 and 1795 the Dorset Justices dealt with over fifty men suspected of carrying false passes and claiming to be distressed seamen.[13] A counterfeit pass cost 3 shillings in London.[14]

The authorities were aware of the problem posed by counterfeiting. That was probably why they printed no fewer than 6,000 passports every year during the 1630s for London constables to use:[15] print could not so easily be copied. It was presumably also why parish officers were supposed to keep registers of vagrants under the 1598 legislation. Few of these registers survive, although a Salisbury volume has been published. Half the vagrants recorded in it were unmarried men; a quarter were single women. Some 20 per cent had travelled over 100 miles: Philip Trume, who had a counterfeit pass and claimed to be a soldier, was punished and sent home to Milford Haven (Pembrokeshire) in 1605. The names of those whipped and given passports may occasionally be found in accounts. There may also be related documents, such as claims by constables for the cost of removing vagrants.

The concept of settlement severely hindered the migration of the labouring population. Parishes were increasingly reluctant to allow potential paupers to become settled within their boundaries. Between 1697 and 1795, a labourer moving to another parish needed a settlement certificate from his home parish. Such certificates would confirm the home parish's liability if relief was needed and would prevent the threat of removal.

Certificates were prepared by churchwardens and overseers and signed by a Justice of the Peace. No record was kept of their issue. Although some recipients retained them, many were surrendered to the overseers of receiving parishes. They were valuable documents, proving settlement if poor relief was claimed without any need for further inquiry. Consequently many were preserved in parish chests. Indeed, sometimes registers of certificates were compiled. At Lacock (Wiltshire), a register was kept briefly, between 1706 and 1709. Of the twelve 'certificate men' listed, one subsequently became churchwarden and thus established his settlement in Lacock.

Certificates usually state the parish in which the migrant was settled and the parish in which he or she intended to live. Sometimes they name family members and perhaps occupations. However, not all parishes were prepared to issue certificates: they were proof that the 'certificate man' was settled in their parish and thus imposed a potential liability on them. Conversely, refusal to issue a certificate might be due to a desire to retain a skilled man in their own parish. The services of tradesmen such as blacksmiths, thatchers and cordwainers were indispensable in self-sufficient communities so their migration had to be prevented if at all possible.

Settlement examinations provide much more information than certificates. When the right of a new migrant to settle was challenged or an applicant for poor relief made his claim, the overseer had to establish his entitlement. Determining 'settlement' was not necessarily an easy task, nor was it a task for the overseer, unless it was obvious. If the pauper had none of the documents mentioned above and was not known to the overseers, he had to be examined under oath, normally by two or more Justices of the Peace. They, or perhaps their clerk, wrote up the results of their inquiry as a settlement examination. Printed forms were sometimes used. Examinations might be retained in parish chests, or sent to the parish of settlement with the pauper and the removal order. A few can be found among Quarter Sessions records. St Clement Danes (London), and possibly other parishes, kept separate registers of examinations.

Settlement examinations provide somewhat biased mini-biographies of the labouring classes. They trace examinees' migration history since they last gained settlements but omit much detail irrelevant to that purpose.

Phrases such as 'he has lived in diverse services' or 'she has served in several places but not for a year' may hide many moves. Examinations do, however, record many events that were relevant to gaining a settlement and enable us to trace the migration patterns of the poor. They are likely to be accurate: a number of Berkshire settlement examinations where the same person was examined twice have been discovered and found to be generally consistent with each other. If there was uncertainty, verification might be sought. The information provided in examinations was likely to include:

- name
- age
- place of birth
- parents' names, occupations and residence
- names of wife and children, with their ages
- occupation(s)
- names and residences of former masters
- details of any apprenticeships served
- former residences.

In 1783 Anthony Davis, a scribbler,[16] was examined before the Bradford on Avon (Wiltshire) magistrates. He was 53 years old and was

'born in Steeple Ashton, where his father James Davis was legally settled. When about 15 years old he was apprenticed by indenture with the consent of his mother (his father being dead) to Jabez Elliott, broadweaver, of Trowbridge, for seven years. Stayed with Elliott in the parish of Trowbridge for seven years. About 18 years ago he was married in Bradford parish church to Hannah his present wife, by whom six children, Susannah 17 years, Hannah 13, Grace 11, Rebecca seven, Isaac five and Sarah two years.'[17]

If the Justices concluded that a pauper's residence lay in another parish, they issued a removal order. These were sometimes written on printed forms, or on the backs of settlement examinations. They were usually acted upon immediately they were made. Removal orders give personal details of the pauper and may include the names of his wife and children. Their primary use to the researcher is the information they give on the removal. Like vagrant's passports, they should have been signed by the constable of each parish through which the pauper passed in order to reach his home parish. Sarah Warman, who was apprehended as a rogue and vagabond in Whitchurch (Shropshire) in 1817, was ordered to be removed to her parish of settlement at Chieveley (Berkshire). It took her a fortnight to reach her destination; probably travelling, under the watchful eye of constables, by carriers' carts.

Removal orders were frequently contested. The courts were clogged up by perpetual war over settlement between parishes. When such disputes took place, parish chests became full of removal orders, notices of appeal, Quarter Sessions orders, accounts from attorneys and related papers. Costs of litigation could be heavy, even exceeding the cost of paying relief. The overseers of Bolney (Sussex) paid over £30 to prove that Brighton was the place of settlement of the Holloway family in 1822. Negotiation was undoubtedly the cheaper method of settling such disputes but parishes frequently adopted xenophobic attitudes towards their neighbours and would not compromise with them.

Removal orders are likely to be found among the records of the parish to which the pauper was removed. Sometimes, an extra copy was made for the original parish.

Removal orders were a last resort; most people threatened with removal would move on if they could before the legal process commenced. Legal removal only affected those who could not move on voluntarily. Indeed, many of those affected moved on before orders could be implemented. Lees has calculated that, on average, fewer than two people were removed from each rural parish each year during the eighteenth and earlier nineteenth centuries.[18]

Identifying a pauper's place of settlement was relatively easy; it was merely necessary to examine the pauper. It was not always so easy to discover who should pay to support a bastard child. Bastardy was a major problem for overseers: as already noted, an illegitimate child had its settlement in the parish where it was born. Its father, however, was legally obliged to support it. Overseers spent a lot of time tracing bastards' fathers and trying to compel them to support their children.

Bastardy examinations of mothers record the efforts of Justices to identify the fathers of illegitimate children. Bastardy bonds record agreements made with fathers to pay maintenance. Both examination and bond are likely to record details of father, mother and child; the bond will also record the amount of maintenance to be paid. Elizabeth Newman, single woman, was examined at Chelsea (Middlesex) in 1734: she made oath that

'she is pregnant of a bastard child or children which was unlawfully begotten on her body by one John Huggett jr. the son of John Huggett of Chelsea … farmer, who had carnal knowledge of her body the first time in the dwelling house of Mr William Burchett of Little Chelsea, farmer, where this examinant lived a hired servant. And several times after in the said house and other out houses belonging to the said Mr Burchett. And this examinant further saith that the said John Huggett jr is the true and only father of the said bastard child or children and that no other person hath had carnal knowledge of her body but the said John Huggett jr.'

Affiliation orders, sometimes written on printed forms, required fathers to pay maintenance. They did not always succeed: at Lacock (Wiltshire), the majority of fathers sooner or later ceased to pay. Perhaps merely a fifth of the expenses incurred were recovered from bastards' fathers.[19] Overseers tried to persuade them to marry the mothers of their children, even going to the lengths of paying them to do so: at Gnosall, John Edge was paid 5 guineas 'for a porshun', and Mr Low was paid 10 shillings 'for marring Edge'. Even the ringers were paid! Thus was the expense of maintaining an illegitimate child avoided.

If the father disappeared, a warrant for his arrest might be issued. Sometimes fathers who evaded arrest for some time found themselves faced with substantial bills for expenses incurred during their absence. In 1821, James Goodall of Hampstead Norreys (Berkshire) was required to pay the massive sum (for a labourer) of over £17 for the lying-in of Hannah Fleetwood and for two years maintenance of twins born in 1819.

Bastardy documents are not generally as informative as settlement examinations; warrants, affiliation orders and bonds rarely provide much information that is not directly relevant to securing maintenance payments from the father. Nevertheless, they are important documents as they establish paternity. They may also tell us something about migration: most fathers were local men but occasionally some lived many miles distant. For example, in Berkshire a few bastards were fathered by men from as far away as London, Essex and Warwick.[20]

Once settlement had been determined and fathers of illegitimate children had been identified, the pauper became eligible for poor relief. However, overseers first had to determine whether he or she owned any goods and, if so, what they were worth. Inventories of paupers' goods could be taken when they claimed relief, or when they died.[21] Overseers might seize those goods to recompense themselves for the cost of relief and needed a record of the goods to be seized. In 1776, the Gnosall (Staffordshire) overseers were ordered 'to take an account of all Paupers goods which may require weekly pay'. It was not only paupers whose goods might be taken: runaway parents, bastards' fathers and absconding tenants could also lose their goods. Inventories can sometimes be found among parish records. They provide good indications of material standards of life among the poor. An example is given in the illustration on p.100.

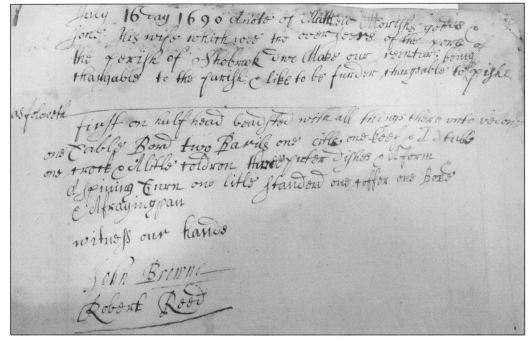

[Inventory of pauper's goods from Shobrooke (Devon). (Devon Record Office 1048A/PS1)

Inventory of a pauper's goods (transcription of illustration)

Jul 16 day 1690. A note of Mathew Moryhs goods & Jone his wife which wee the overseers of the pore of the parish of Shobrook dwo make our reentear : being chargable to the parish & like to be furder chargeable to pishe

as foloweth

First on half head beadsted with all things there unto belong, one table bord two barils one citle one keef & old table one crock & a little coldron three puter dishes & a form a spining turn one little standerd one coffer one boxe & a fraying pan

Witness our hands

John Browne

Robert Reed

From Devon Record Office 1048A/PS1

Payment of poor relief between 1597 and 1834 was a matter for overseers, under the supervision of Justices of the Peace. After 1834, their responsibilities were much diminished, but they continued to distribute relief in certain circumstances. Their disbursements are recorded in accounts. Overseers' accounts provide a huge amount of detail concerning parish life. Paupers had to be fed, clothed, housed and provided with fuel. Costs of enforcement action had to be met.

The idea that the poor should be set to work was appealing and was included in the Elizabethan legislation. Generally, however, this was not successful; many work schemes were tried and failed. On the other hand, there may have been many informal work schemes requiring no expenditure and therefore unrecorded. Some overseers required farmers to employ their paupers on a rota system. This system is recorded in Lacock (Wiltshire) between 1829 and 1831, as the farmers paid wages to the overseers who then paid the paupers.

Despite the lack of success, attempts to provide work continued to be made into the eighteenth and nineteenth centuries. Parishes sometimes built their own workhouses. The poor house at Lacock, hitherto used to accommodate a few pauper families, was converted into a workhouse for children in 1758.

An Act of 1723 authorized parishes to join together to provide workhouses. Over 100 workhouses were built within a decade under this act.[22] In 1776, sixty parishes in Norfolk came together to establish a 'house of industry' at Gressinghall. By 1777 there were almost 2,000 workhouses in England, although by then it was appreciated that they were generally not able to pay their way as economic units.[23] They did, however, drive down the numbers of poor who wanted to claim relief. Life in the workhouse was not an attractive prospect.

In one respect, the work clauses of the Elizabethan legislation did succeed. Pauper apprenticeship gave work to many thousands of children and offered a long-term solution to the problem of what to do with them. The cost of an apprenticeship premium was outweighed by the expense of paying poor relief for several years.

Apprenticeship was the means by which society trained the younger generation in the trades needed to earn their living. The apprentice was expected to live in his master's house for seven years while learning his trade. His master provided food, lodging, clothes, laundry, medical care if necessary, and acted *in loco parentis* towards his apprentice. The two parties entered into indentures and, on completion of the term, the apprentice became eligible to become a freeman of his guild and of the borough, entitled to trade in his own right. Private apprentices were usually young teenagers when they were bound. Occasionally, private indentures were deposited in parish chests for safe-keeping. These are likely to record the names of apprentices, usually the names of fathers (or widowed mothers), perhaps fathers' occupations and perhaps their parishes of residence.

Pauper apprenticeship was a perversion of this system. It was, admittedly, a means of providing poor relief, but it was also a disciplinary measure. According to one contemporary, pauper apprenticeship was intended 'not for the education of boys in arts, but for charity to keep them and relieve them from turning to roguery and idleness'.[24] The origins of pauper apprenticeship date back to before the 1597 legislation: at Great Bentley (Essex) the earliest apprenticeship indenture dates from 1578. The possibility of apprenticing pauper children was seized on by overseers as a valuable solution to their problem. The 1,526 children bound out by Hertfordshire parish overseers in 1619 constituted perhaps 30 per cent of children aged between 7 and 16 in the county.[25] Indentures continued to be written until the nineteenth century.

Overseers could apprentice pauper children without reference to their parents, who could only prevent such bindings by withdrawing their claim to poor relief. Until 1816, children could be bound at a very young age,

The apprenticeship indentures of Richard Burgess of Heavitree, 1778.
(Devon Record Office 3004A)

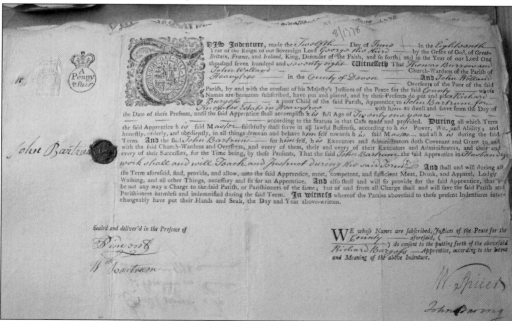

perhaps 5 or 6. Masters could be compelled to accept pauper apprentices, facing a fine for refusal. The statutory penalty was £10. A boy who was difficult to place could earn his parish a substantial amount of money: in Leeds (Yorkshire), the vestry had an annual income of over £1,000 from such fines.

Apprenticeship premiums were sometimes funded from fines. The Heavitree (Devon) overseers regularly paid an 'assignment fee' of 20 shillings from 1820. In 1676–7 the Gedling (Nottinghamshire) overseers paid William Smalley 13s 4d 'concerning Patience Moreley that was imposed upon him Apprentice'. Others, on the edge of poverty themselves, accepted an apprentice purely for the sake of the premium and ignored their responsibilities towards the apprentice. Overseers were keen to find masters in other parishes. Apprentices' settlement depended upon their masters' settlement. By placing an apprentice outside their own parish, overseers ensured that they would not have to pay him relief in future.

The 'trades' to which paupers were apprenticed frequently did not lead to a secure future. 'Husbandry' for boys and 'housewifery' for girls frequently meant drudgery, without learning a useful trade. In towns, chimney-sweeps were keen to recruit small boys who could climb chimneys; not a skill that they could carry forward into adult life. In the late eighteenth century, the growth of the textile industry in northern England brought with it demands for cheap labour to man the new factories. Pauper apprentices provided a ready supply of such labour, although the conditions under which they worked were not those of traditional apprenticeship. A factory apprentice rarely ate at his master's table or slept under his roof. The personal relationship between master and apprentice that had been the hallmark of the old system did not exist in the same way in northern factories. Indeed, the existing personal relationships of apprentices suffered: they could easily lose contact with their parents if their workplace was distant from their home. The apprenticeship of London children at a distance greater than 40 miles away was prohibited in 1815.

The chief record of pauper apprenticeship is the indenture. This recorded the agreement between the overseers and the master. Many pauper indentures can be found among parish records.

The wording of pauper indentures was established by statute. In the eighteenth and nineteenth centuries, printed forms were frequently used. Indentures open with the date and the names of the parties. The agreement was between the master and the overseers. They record the master's name and perhaps identify his wife, his parish and his trade. Overseers are named individually. Neither the pauper nor his parents were parties. The pauper was named but not his parents, who had no legal rights in the binding.

The indenture is likely to specify the trade that the apprentice was to learn, sometimes the premium to be paid to the master, and the term. The premium was likely to be small, perhaps £5. Pauper premiums may be mentioned in overseers' accounts and in apprenticeship registers (see below).

Pauper apprentices served their masters for much longer than private apprentices. They were originally required to serve until they were 24, at least in the case of boys. This was reduced to age 21 in 1766 (London) and 1778 (nationally). Girls only had to serve until age 21 or their earlier marriage. Masters were expected to provide all 'necessaries' and sometimes agreed to provide two suits of clothes, or made other provision, at the end of the term.

Indentures were prepared in duplicate on a single sheet, separated along an indented line. In case of dispute the two copies could be authenticated by being joined together again. The master signed one copy, giving it to the overseers; the overseers signed the other, giving it to the master.

Pauper indentures are frequently found with binding orders signed by two Justices of the Peace. These orders were necessitated by an Act of 1816, requiring Justices to ensure that masters were fit and proper persons and that they did not live more than 40 miles from the pauper's home parish. This Act also prevented the apprenticeship of children under 9 years of age.

Registers of pauper apprentices were kept by overseers, from 1766 in London and from 1802 elsewhere. Poor Law Unions took over this responsibility in 1844. Printed books, in a format laid down by legislation, were usually used. They record the names, sex, ages and parents of apprentices. They also name masters, their trades and their residences, stating the premium paid and the term of the apprenticeship. The names of overseers, and of the Justices who assented to bindings, are also given. These registers may be more useful than the indentures since, unlike the latter, they include details of parents.

Much information about pauper apprentices is found in vestry minutes. The vestry of St Olave Hart Street (London), for example, ordered in 1706–07 that 'Rd Elton's daughter be put to Prentice to Mrs Marjoram a child's cote maker Liveing in Dorsett Street in Spittle Fields'. In 1830, the Shobrooke (Devon) vestry voted to establish new 'rules or mode of binding apprentices'. Apprentices were to be allocated to ratepayers in proportion to the rates they paid. For example, if they paid between 10d and 12½d they were liable to accept five apprentices.

The cost of binding apprentices was met by overseers, and was recorded in their accounts. In 1622, for example, the overseers of Paris Garden, Southwark (Surrey) paid out £4 10s 'to putt out John Clemens to be prentic vnto John Cragges'. Sometimes apprentices were bound to their fathers: in

1821 the Gnosall (Staffordshire) overseers paid 10 shillings to 'John Smith to teach his son the trade of a shoemaker'.

Many apprentices ran away from their masters, failing to complete their terms. Frequently this was due to ill treatment. It was possible for Justices of the Peace to cancel indentures when this occurred. One instance of a cancellation is recorded among the indentures of Gnosall.

Another means of relieving the poor was to export them to the colonies, where they could supposedly maintain themselves. In 1831, the Lacock (Wiltshire) vestry voted to borrow £500 'to defray the passage of such persons as may be disposed to emigrate to Canada'. In 1838, the Kettering (Northamptonshire) vestry resolved to create a fund to pay 'the expenses of emigration of poor persons having settlements in this parish and being willing to emigrate'.

It was sometimes cheaper simply to provide the means by which the poor could earn their own living. Sometimes overseers paid them to look after young orphans before they could be apprenticed, to provide lodging for more mature paupers or to nurse the sick. At the end of the eighteenth century, Mary Frost of Hooton Pagnell (Yorkshire) was given 'a new wheel' to enable her to spin wool.

Regular pensions were only paid under rigorous conditions. Pensioners were expected to attend church regularly, to be industrious and sober, to show deference to their 'betters' and to take seriously the duties of parenthood. An Act of 1692 required overseers to keep a register of regular pensioners, recording when relief was first paid and 'the occasion which brought him under that necessity'. The register was to be shown to the vestry annually and 'all persons receiving collections to be called over and the reasons of their taking relief examined'. New regular pensions could only be paid under the authority of a Justice of the Peace. In Lacock (Wiltshire), the list of pensioners for 1722 includes eleven who were 'old infirm and impotent', one 'old and blind', two 'lame' or 'old and lame', one 'a natural' and one 'bedridden'. Two needed relief due to the size of their families, two children had lame fathers and a third was 'fatherless and motherless'. Dependence on the parish could sometimes last a long time, typically between five and twelve years, although at Cowden (Kent) Goodwife Wells was on the parish for no less than thirty-six years. The number of pensioners increased dramatically during the eighteenth century. In Lacock there had been only twenty-two in 1722; by the end of the century there was an average of sixty-three. In the early nineteenth century there were even more; an average of c125 in the first quarter of the century.

By the early nineteenth century, more energetic vestries were appointing a salaried overseer who could visit the poor in their homes to check up on their need for relief. Some even went to the length of publishing lists of paupers. Lists published by the St Asaph (Denbighshire) vestry were said to have frequently brought 'to light cases of imposture which otherwise would have remained undetected'.[26]

Some vestries privatized the relief of the poor. In 1812, the Chalfont St Peter (Buckinghamshire) vestry paid a contractor £812 and gave him the use of the parish workhouse. In return, he met the entire cost of poor relief for the year. The contract, together with those for most of the years between 1800 and 1833 is among the parish records.

A wide variety of expenditure could be incurred. Housing the poor was a priority. Habitation orders issued by Justices proliferated in the late seventeenth century; overseers were required to provide accommodation.[27] Rents were frequently paid, sometimes in addition to paupers' weekly pay. At Hadleigh (Suffolk), between 1579 and 1596 no fewer than sixty-three paupers were billeted on householders, two-thirds of them children.[28] The Chalfont St Peter's church house was used to accommodate the poor; in 1725/6 the overseers paid £5 rent to the churchwardens. At Hooton Pagnell (Yorkshire) a number of cottages were rented, each for occupation by several unrelated paupers.

Orphans were usually boarded out until they could be apprenticed. In 1592, Chagford (Devon) churchwardens paid various sums for the maintenance of pauper children. William Lopaz, Agnis Throuston and Richard Westawaie received 22s 4d 'of Otte's child', presumably for board. Another 6 pence was spent on 'a pair of shoes for the same child'.

Clothing the poor was an essential aspect of overseers' work. Their accounts can be invaluable sources for the history of clothing. St Clement Danes (London) kept clothing books, giving details of the clothing issued to each pauper. It cost the overseers of Gnosall (Staffordshire) 10 shillings to purchase John Stafford two pairs of shoes in 1682. They also paid out 8 shillings for leather, 2s 8d for 'thred and buttons' and the same amount 'for makeing his Clothes'. Margaret Davies subsequently had 4 pence for washing them.

An Act of 1697 required paupers to be badged: the badge had to carry a red 'P', together with the initial of the parish. Its purpose was to emphasize that claiming relief was a mark not only of dependency but also of humiliation. The vestry of St Olave Hart Street (London) 'Orderd that the Church Wardens do provide Badges for ye poor of ye Parish & yt no Pensioner be allowed any alms or Pension that doth not constantly wear ye said Badge' in 1728. Refusal to wear a badge could mean no relief: the 1729 accounts of Chalfont St Peter (Buckinghamshire) record: 'Widow Dell no bodge this month no pay.' However, the rule was not consistently enforced.

Keeping paupers warm in the winter was also important. The overseers of Paris Garden, Southwark (Surrey) purchased coal every year in the seventeenth century, presumably for this purpose; in 1658 it cost them over £90. At Hooton Pagnell (Yorkshire) 'one dozen of coals' was regularly purchased for the poor in the eighteenth century.

Caring for the sick poor was another expense. Doctors' bills were frequently recorded in accounts. In 1743/4, the overseers of Chalfont St Peter (Buckinghamshire) paid 3 guineas for 'Doctor Millsh bill for Chipses broken leg'. Accidents are constantly recorded. In 1821, the Gnosall (Staffordshire) overseers gave 12 shillings to John Proudman, 'unable to work in consequence of being shot by Mr Bull, sadler'. Nursing was another frequent expense: 4 shillings was paid in Gnosall in 1694 to 'Butchers wife for looking to Davies family when sick (small pox)'. Looking after them would have been dangerous and was therefore well-paid; one hopes she did not catch the disease. When Lacock (Wiltshire) suffered a severe epidemic of smallpox in 1776, the vestry experimented with a new remedy: they paid Dr Banks 23 shillings for inoculating the poor. The experiment appears to have been successful and the same remedy was adopted when the disease appeared again.

Nursing care was frequently provided by families, with the parish helping out. In 1767, the overseers of Hooton Pagnell (Yorkshire) agreed that Nicholas Wilkinson was to be cared for by his two sons, who were to be paid 2 shillings weekly 'so long as he shall live'.

Sometimes the sick had to be institutionalized. The mid-eighteenth century overseers of Chalfont St Peter (Buckinghamshire) rented a pesthouse – a converted barn – where the sick were tended. When George Monk went mad in 1739, he had to be sent to Bedlam. The cost amounted to more than 10s. He was subsequently brought home but spent the rest of his life in and out of the village cage.

Death also incurred expense. The overseers of Westbury on Trym (Gloucestershire) gave 2 shillings to 'Jane Jeffiries for tending her mother'. She was subsequently given 6 shillings 'towards the buring of her mother'. Similarly 'Ottes' child' at Chagford (Devon), whom we have already met, required 'a shroud' costing 12 pence. The cost of paupers' deaths fell on the parish: in 1697 at Gnosall, Mr Samuel Ffowke, as churchwarden, paid himself 1s 6d 'for fetching Thomas Lightwood to Church from Knightley he being dead in the snow'. It is always worth checking overseers' accounts for deaths if they cannot be found elsewhere.

In addition to their own poor, parishes had to provide support for travellers passing through. Vagrants with passes could legitimately claim relief, but they were only a minority. A few others – less than 10 per cent –

were whipped.[29] Many were simply given a night's lodging and sent on their way. Travellers of higher status sometimes received greater assistance. Cratfield (Suffolk) paid 2 shillings 'to William King, a minister, who was driven out of Ireland from his benefice by the rebells' in 1642. This was not the only amount they paid to those who suffered during the conflict, and rebels were not the only enemy. The Upton (Nottinghamshire) constable's accounts record relief being 'Given to a sea fayring man … which were taken captive by ye turkes & utterlye depryved of all his goodes to the value of £450, as it did appeare by his testimonial & also beinge greevouslye maimed of his bodye.'

Most responsibility for relieving paupers passed to Poor Law Union guardians in 1834. However, overseers retained a number of minor responsibilities and the names of paupers still appeared in their accounts. Overseers could order paupers to be admitted to Union workhouses, and lists of those so admitted may survive. There may also continue to be lists of paupers relieved by the overseers.[30]

Overseers had to find the wherewithal to support paupers. In the sixteenth and seventeenth centuries heavy reliance was placed on voluntary contributions, although overseers were entitled to levy a poor rate. At Allhallows Lombard Street (London), voluntary contributions totalled up to £24 annually in the early seventeenth century.[31] That was in addition to a compulsory poor rate. Occasionally collections were taken for individuals: when the curate of St Dunstan in the West (London) died in 1633, the parishioners collected no less than £112 to support his destitute widow and five small children. Money might also be borrowed. There is a 'note of the names of those that doth lend money to biy corne to the use of the poore' in the Lacock (Wiltshire) accounts during the famine year of 1595.

The importance of rates steadily increased. Originally, much poor relief was funded by bequests of lands to the parish, collections in church and other charitable activity. Rates were seen as a second best, despite Charles I's injunction that the availability of charity was to be 'no occasion of lessening the rates of the parish'.[32] Many overseers continued to use property bequeathed to the poor to keep the rates down. However, by 1660 well over a third of parishes were levying compulsory poor rates and by the end of the century they were universal.[33]

Rates had to be approved by two Justices of the Peace. Legally, the vestry had no say in the matter. However, usually overseers' accounts were placed before the vestry as well as being seen by the Justices. The names of those liable to pay and the amounts due from them are likely to be recorded in overseers' accounts or in separate rate books.

Poor rates continued to be levied by overseers until 1925. Auditing was tightened-up in the nineteenth century: Hugh Owen's *Manual for Overseers, Assistant Overseers, Collectors of Poor Rates, and Vestry Clerks* (5th ed., Knight & Co., 1880) devotes much space to the procedures to be followed. Overseers were required to keep no fewer than seven different types of accounting books. The valuation lists they compiled up until 1925 list all ratepayers.

Vestry minutes contain much information concerning the poor, and vestries played a major role in determining assessments to poor rates. The vestry minutes of Gnosall (Staffordshire) record many disputes over assessment. The principle was that if a ratepayer's assessment was reduced following an appeal, another ratepayer's assessment had to be increased. In 1690, for example, it is recorded that 'John Congreve abated 4d layd upon Henry Hall 3d Thos Pooler 1d'.

Major initiatives were likely to come before the vestry. For example, the vestry established a poor house at Wandsworth (Surrey) as early as 1558. In 1716, a committee of the vestry of St Giles Cripplegate were meeting to discuss the provision of workhouses in each part of the parish. Some boroughs, such as Bristol (1696) and Exeter (1698), established Corporations of the Poor to take over the administration of the Poor Law from parish officers.

Disputes over settlement are regularly recorded: the Cholesbury (Buckinghamshire) vestry resolved in 1834 'that legal proceedings be forthwith taken against the late overseers of Tring for having conspired to bring about the marriage of Cripple Cox to a pauper of their parish'. Tring (Hertfordshire) evidently hoped to fix their pauper's settlement in Cholesbury.

More personal matters, such as the punishment of wayward girls, might also be brought before the vestry. At Otterton (Devon) in 1764, it was

> 'agreed at a parish meeting by us the parishioners who were then present, that the Churchwardens shall take out an Order of Penance against Pascho Potter who was presented at the last visitation of a Bad child, and that the expenses of it be allowed and reinfurced then either out of the poor or Church Rate.'

The last clause is worth noting: although church and poor rates were technically separate, it was not always clear which should be used for a particular expense.

In principle, where overseers' accounts record expenses concerning the removal of paupers, there should also be a removal order and a settlement

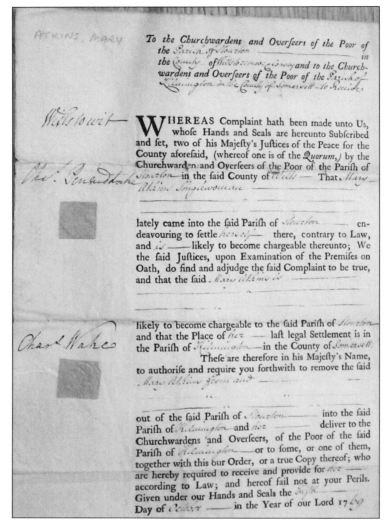

Order to remove Mary Atkins from Stourton (Wiltshire).
(Wiltshire & Swindon History Centre 1240/26)

examination. There might also have been a hearing before Quarter Sessions. It is worth checking for all these documents; however, it is frequently the case that not all have survived. For example, between 1784 and 1800 there are twenty-seven entries in the overseers' accounts of Ifield (Sussex) but no removal orders.

Many parishes kept registers of paupers, following an Act of 1691. Immediately after the Act, the Gnosall (Staffordshire) vestry ordered compliance with it. Registers of paupers in receipt of relief were maintained by St Clement Danes (London) from 1733. At St Dionis Backchurch, probably uniquely, a 'workhouse inquest register' was kept, recording visits to the workhouse by churchwardens and overseers and noting any complaints from inmates.

In 1762 a further Act was passed 'for the keeping regular, uniform and annual Registers, of all Parish Poor Infants under a certain Age'. At first, only children under the age of 4 were covered; however, an Act of 1766 extended the age range to 14 and, as has been seen, required a separate register of pauper apprentices. These Acts only covered certain parishes in the London area but the resultant registers are invaluable sources, providing extensive details of pauper children.

A wide range of other documentation regarding the poor can also be found. Many letters from overseers survive and some for Sussex have been printed. Sokoll's edition of *Essex Pauper Letters* includes over 1,000 pieces of correspondence. The majority are written by paupers who were not living in their parish of settlement: if they had been, they would not have needed to write. Others are written on behalf of paupers by diligent clergymen, benevolent masters, close relatives and even the overseers of host parishes. Most pauper letters display a rhetoric of deferential gratitude, although they make it clear that they felt entitled to claim relief. They were generally appealing to officialdom to relieve their pressing needs. Many, however, stray from their primary purpose and make irrelevant asides that provide valuable information for researchers. They tell us a great deal concerning the circumstances of the poor.

Arrest warrants, and warrants ordering overseers to pay poor relief, are frequently found. So are accounts from other parishes related to expenses incurred in undertaking pauper removals. If a parish had a workhouse, then there may be lists of inmates and other workhouse administrative documents.

Much can be learned from overseers' archives about social attitudes and relationships, employment patterns and migration. Topics such as hiring customs, clothing and housing are covered in detail. Poor Law records also enable us to explore the attitudes and activities of the poor themselves. The family historian can have a field day tracing ancestors' apprenticeships, migrations, unemployment and illnesses.

Further Reading
For good general introductions to the history of the Poor Law, see:
• Hindle, Steve. *On the Parish?: The Micro-Politics of Poor Relief in Rural England c.1550–1750.* (Clarendon Press, 2004).

- Lees, Lynn Hollen. *The Solidarities of Strangers: The English Poor Laws and the People, 1700–1948.* (Cambridge University Press, 1998).

For vagrants, see:

- Eccles, Audrey. *Vagrancy in Law and Practice under the Old Poor Law* (Ashgate, 2012).
- Beier, A.L. *Masterless Men: The Vagrancy Pattern in England 1560–1642.* (Methuen, 1985).

On the law of settlement, see:

- Taylor, J.S. *Poverty, Migration, and Settlement in the Industrial Revolution: Sojourners' Narratives.* (Society for the Promotion of Science and Scholarship, 1989).

Basic introductions to Poor Law records are provided by:

- Fowler, Simon. *Poor Law Records for Family Historians.* (Family History Partnership, 2011).
- Cole, Anne. *An Introduction to Poor Law Documents Before 1834.* 2nd ed. (Federation of Family History Societies, 2000).

For a more detailed guide, see:

- Burlison, Robert. *Tracing Your Pauper Ancestors: A Guide for Family Historians.* (Pen & Sword, 2009).

Many facsimiles of Poor Law documents are printed in:

- Hawkings, David T. *Pauper Ancestors: A Guide to the Records Created by the Poor Laws in England and Wales.* (History Press, 2011).

Guides to settlement papers and overseers' accounts are included in:

- Thompson, K.M. *Short Guides to Records, Second series guides: 25–48.* (Historical Association, 1997).

A detailed guide to apprenticeship records – pauper, charity and private – is provided by:

- Raymond, Stuart A. *My Ancestor was an Apprentice: How Can I Find Out More About Him?* (Society of Genealogists, 2010).

For pauper letters, see:

- King, Steven. 'Pauper Letters as a Source', *Family & Community History* 10(2), 2007, pp.167–70.
- Levene, Alysa, et al, eds. *Narratives of the Poor in Eighteenth-Century Britain.* Vol. 1: *Voices of the Poor: Poor Law Depositions and Letters.* Pickering & Chatto, 2006.

BEDFORDSHIRE

- Emmison, F.G. 'Poor Relief Accounts of Two Rural Parishes in Bedfordshire 1563, 1598', *Economic History Review* 3, 1950, pp.102–16.

BERKSHIRE

- Durrant, Peter, ed. *Berkshire Overseers' Papers, 1654–1834.* Berkshire Record Society 3, 1997.

BUCKINGHAMSHIRE

- Edmonds, Geoffrey C. 'Accounts of Eighteenth-Century Overseers of the Poor of Chalfont St Giles', *Records of Buckinghamshire*, 18(1), 1966, pp.3–23.

ESSEX

- Sokoll, Thomas, ed. *Essex Pauper Letters, 1731–1837*, Records of Social and Economic History, new series 30. (Oxford University Press, 2001).

GLOUCESTERSHIRE

- Gray, Irvine, ed. *Cheltenham Settlement Examinations, 1815–1826* (Bristol & Gloucestershire Archaeological Society Records Section 7. 1969).
- Wilkins, H.J., ed. *Transcriptions of the Poor Book of the Tithings of Westbury on Trym, Stoke Bishop, and Shirehampton, from A.D. 1656–1698, with Introduction and Notes.* (J.W. Arrowsmith, 1910).

HAMPSHIRE

- Willis, Arthur J. ed. *Winchester Settlement Papers 1667–1842, from Records of Several Winchester Parishes.* (Self-published, 1967).

LANCASHIRE

- Hindle, G.B. *Provision for the Relief of the Poor in Manchester 1754–1826* (Chetham Society 3rd series 23, 1976). Useful bibliography.

MIDDLESEX

- Hitchcock, Tim & Black, John, eds. *Chelsea Settlement and Bastardy Examinations, 1733–1766.* (London Record Society 33, 1999), p.6.

STAFFORDSHIRE

- Cutlack, S.A., ed. 'The Gnosall Records 1679 to 1837: Poor Law Administration', *Collections for the History of Staffordshire 1936*, pp.1–141.

SURREY

- Norman, Philip. 'The Accounts of the Overseers of the Poor of Paris Garden, Southwark, 17 May 1608 to 30 September 1671', *Surrey Archaeological Collections* 16, 1901, pp.55–136.

SUSSEX

- Pilbeam, Norma & Nelson, Ian, eds. *Poor Law Records of Mid-Sussex 1601–1835.* (Sussex Record Society 83, 1999).

WILTSHIRE

- Hembry, Phyllis, ed. *Calendar of Bradford on Avon Settlement Examinations and Removal Orders 1725–98.* (Wiltshire Record Society 46, 1990).
- Slack, Paul, ed. *Poverty in Early Stuart Salisbury.* (Wiltshire Record Society 31, 1975).
- Hinton, F.H. 'Notes on the Administration of the Relief of the Poor of Lacock, 1583 to 1834', *Wiltshire Magazine* 49, 1940–42, pp.166–218.

Chapter 5

RECORDS RELATING TO THE CHURCH

Parish records include a wide variety of records relating to the church building, the clergy, worship and the glebe. Inventories of church goods, glebe terriers, faculties for alterations to the fabric, seating plans, Easter offering books and registers of preachers and services all tell us something about the church building and its furnishing, the people who sat in the pews, and the way in which the daily routine of worship was conducted.

Inventories of Church Goods

Most parishes had inventories made of the goods they possessed. These may be separate documents, but may also be found written into a variety of books such as registers and accounts. They formed a useful means of holding churchwardens to account for the goods of the church. Archdeacons expected to view inventories during their visitations. The earliest post-Reformation inventory for Tavistock (Devon), dated 1561–2, is written into the churchwardens' accounts for this purpose. Throughout the eighteenth century, Liverpool churchwardens compiled inventories every year.

Inventories reveal the wealth or poverty of churches and the wide range of vessels, cloth, furniture and other possessions used in worship. Pre-Reformation inventories may record the relics of saints: Allhallows, London Wall, had 'a bone of Saynt Davy closed in sylver' in 1525. The printed accounts of St Peters (Hertfordshire) include an inventory of 1586 listing the cloths, pots and books kept in the vestry, together with a list of 'Debtes owinge and dewe to the Church'. Some of the goods held were 'in the custodye of William Hickman' and were labelled 'venditum'; presumably they were to be sold to help pay off the debts.

The best-known inventories are those compiled during the Reformation to facilitate the seizure of property used for 'superstitious' purposes. Commissions to make inventories of church goods were first issued in 1549. Others followed: in 1552 new inventories were ordered and in January 1553 commissioners were ordered to seize all church valuables. Only the bare minimum was to be left for the conduct of services. This process was halted in midstream when Edward died and was succeeded by Mary: she attempted to return the plate already seized to the parishes.

The inventories compiled in this process were written as indentures, one part of which was retained by the parish (few copies survive). The other portion was returned to the Exchequer. Many inventories and other documents from this process are now in The National Archives, class E117.[1]

In the Hundred of West (Cornwall), and probably elsewhere, these inventories were compiled by 'the parsons, vicars, curates, churchwardens and other discreet persons'.[2] The actual questions put to compilers have not been recorded but their tenor can be worked out from the replies. Cresswell suggests that the questions put to the Exeter (Devon) churchwardens were as follows:

1. Can you affirm that this is a true inventory of your church goods?
2. Have you any other inventory?
3. What plate have you?
4. What vestments have you?
5. How many bells have you?
6. From what evidence have you drawn up this inventory?
7. Was there ever any other inventory?
8. In what form were the church goods put into your charge?
9. Has anyone received any part of your church goods?
10. Have any of them been removed?
11. Has anything been sold?
12. Have any of them been stolen?
13. Are there fewer than formerly?
14. What is the weight of your plate?

The Commissioners were obviously alive to the possibility of concealment, but were not always successful in preventing it, as has already been seen in the case of Morebath (Devon). They did, however, discover that an astute mayor of Exeter had persuaded the city's parishes to donate much of their plate towards the construction of the canal. The city was allowed to retain it, but only after much angst, and probably only in view of the city's loyalty during the 1549 Rebellion.

Surviving inventories do not necessarily list all church goods; quite apart from the problem of concealment, their primary purpose was to identify those goods that were worth seizing. Some only mention plate (such as chalices and crosses) and bells. The Newnham Murren (Oxfordshire) churchwardens reported merely a 'chalic of sylver' and '3 belles'. Indeed, some churches compiled inventories of goods other than those reported to the Commissioners: at Baldock (Hertfordshire) there is 'an inventory of old stuffe besides the Kynges Inventory' dated 1553. The Baldock churchwardens evidently took the opportunity of listing the 'old' vestments, linen, brass and iron which they had thought unnecessary to include in the inventory compiled for the Commissioners. Other churchwardens sometimes recorded such goods in the official inventories. One test of comprehensiveness that can be applied is to compare inventories with the lists of goods returned to churches by the Marian regime (which are also in E117). In Cornwall, these show little correlation with the Edwardian inventories.

Further Reading
The Edwardian inventories are discussed in:
- 'The End of it All: The Material Culture of the Late Medieval English Parish and the 1552 Inventories of Church Goods', in Duffy, Eamon, *Saints, Sacrilege and Tradition: Religion and Conflict in the Tudor Reformations.* (Bloomsbury, 2012), pp.109–32.

Many Edwardian inventories have been published. See, for example:

BEDFORDSHIRE
- Eeles, F.C., ed. *The Edwardian Inventories for Bedfordshire.* (Alcuin Club Collections 6, 1905).

BUCKINGHAMSHIRE
- Eeles, F.C., ed. *The Edwardian Inventories for Buckinghamshire.* (Alcuin Club Collections 9, 1908).

CORNWALL
- Snell, Lawrence S. *The Edwardian Inventories of Church Goods for Cornwall.* (1955)

DEVON
- Cresswell, Beatrix S., ed. *The Edwardian Inventories for the City and County of Exeter.* (Alcuin Club Collections 20, 1916).

HERTFORDSHIRE
- Cussans, J.E., ed. *Inventory of Furniture and Ornaments Remaining in all the Parish Churches of Hertfordshire in the Last Year of the Reign of King Edward the Sixth.* (James Parker, 1873).

HUNTINGDONSHIRE
- Lomas, S.C., ed. *The Edwardian Inventories for Huntingdonshire* (Alcuin Club Collections 7, 1906).

OXFORDSHIRE
- Graham, Rose, ed. *The Chantry Certificates … and the Edwardian Inventories of Church Goods.* (Oxfordshire Record Society 1, 1919). Also issued as (Alcuin Club Collections 23, 1920).

- Page, W., ed. *The Inventories of Church Goods for the Counties of York, Durham, and Northumberland.* (Surtees Society 97, 1896).

Bede Rolls

In most pre-Reformation churches, the names of deceased benefactors of the church were listed in a bede roll. It enabled their souls to be prayed for, either from the pulpit or privately. Most rolls were destroyed during the Reformation. There are, however, a few rare survivors. A fragmentary copy of the mid-fifteenth-century roll from St Mary's, Sandwich (Kent) survives.[3] The list of benefactors in the church book of All Saints, Bristol, covering the period c.1480–1510, may have served as a bede roll, regularly read at Sunday services. Entries on the bede roll were frequently paid for: the early sixteenth-century churchwardens' accounts of Stratton (Cornwall) record that a substantial proportion of their income came from payments made for being entered on the bede roll, for which the standard fee was 3s 4d. There were so many names listed that it is unlikely the roll was read at weekly services; more probably it was just read on All Souls' Day and displayed so that the faithful could pray privately. At Spurriergate, York, many early sixteenth-century benefactors left money or property to pay for masses for their souls.

Glebe Terriers

Glebe terriers provide detailed descriptions of the way in which particular benefices were funded. The glebe was the land assigned as part of a parish priest's living. The word 'terrier' is derived from the Latin *terra* (earth). The prime purpose of these terriers was to protect the rights and property of the incumbent against dispute and encroachment.

The origin of terriers is generally dated to a 1571 canon in which Archbishop Parker instructed his bishops to 'see that true inventories, which are called terriers, of all fields, meadows, gardens and orchards belonging to Rectories or Vicarages, be made by the inspection of honest men, and sent to his registry, as a perpetual reminder'.[4] Some bishops responded promptly: terriers from the Diocese of Gloucester were compiled in 1572 and others followed in succeeding years.[5] Generally, however, compilation only took place when it was ordered by the bishop, usually during an episcopal visitation, and in most dioceses surviving terriers can be dated to these visitations. In the Diocese of Exeter, for example, they generally survive from 1601, 1613, 1679–80, 1726–7 and 1746.[6] In the Diocese of Lincoln they are much more frequent; they were compiled for every triennial visitation.

Canon 87 of 1603–04 made the canon of 1571 more explicit:

'… the archbishop and all bishops within their several dioceses shall procure (as much as in them lieth) that a true note and terrier of all the glebes, lands, meadows, gardens, orchards, houses, stocks, implements, tenements, and portions of tithes, lying out of their parishes (which belong to any parsonage or vicarage, or rural prebend) be taken by the view of honest men in every parish, by the appointment of the bishop (whereof the minister to be one), and be laid up in the bishop's registry, there to be a perpetual memory thereof.'

The final instruction indicates the resting-place of most glebe terriers: the diocesan registry (now usually the local record office).

Copies of terriers can, nevertheless, be found among parish records, although many have been lost. In 1710, the Lower House of Convocation suggested that one copy should be made for the parish chest. Visitation articles frequently enquired whether previous terriers were held and copies were frequently written into registers or accounts. The terrier for Gwennap (Cornwall) in the diocesan registry notes that it was copied into the parish register, where it was signed. At St Chad's, Shrewsbury, a summary of the 1751 terrier was painted on a board and hung in the church.

The information recorded in glebe terriers varies over time, between dioceses (dependent on the bishops' instructions) and also between parishes. In Warwickshire, the details to be included were left to the discretion of the incumbent and churchwardens. By contrast, in 1605–6 the Diocese of Lincoln employed William Folkingham as 'general surveyor of church gleabes'. He established a format for terriers that was followed by every parish in the following years, and is indeed named in them. In Berkshire Dr Nicholas Tooker, the Archdeacon's official, played a major role in ensuring that terriers were compiled during the metropolitical visitation of 1634.

At first terriers only dealt with the glebe land and the parsonage house. The 1603–4 canon barely mentioned tithe, despite its importance. It was, however, quickly realized that details of tithing customs, parish boundaries, charities, church goods and a variety of other topics could all usefully be recorded in the terrier. Place-name researchers may discover incidental mention of many minor place names, sometimes recorded nowhere else.

Glebe terriers usually commence by describing the glebe, noting its extent, cropping and the names of neighbouring landowners. Gardens, orchards, arable fields, meadows, pasture and woodland are all mentioned. Maintaining a record of glebe lands was particularly important in parishes where there were open fields and where strips of glebe in them could easily be encroached upon. Exchanges of land are occasionally mentioned, as are disputes. At St

Erth (Cornwall), glebe had been 'for some considerable space of Time detained from the Church by the force & strength of Sir John Kelligrew'. It had, however, been recovered. The church of Honington (Warwickshire) was not so fortunate: property worth 40 shillings per annum intended 'for the reparacion & vse of the Church' had 'beene taken away for the space of fortie yeares last past, & are now in the possession of Sr Henry Gibs'.

The glebe included the parsonage house and its outbuildings. When Bishop Barrington of Salisbury ordered the compilation of terriers in 1783, his first instruction to his diocesan clergy and churchwardens was to 'describe the parsonage or Vicarage-House': the number of rooms, the building materials and 'manner they are floored, wainscoted and cieled' all had to be noted. When such instructions were followed, terriers provide us with a valuable source of information on vernacular architecture. Detailed information on the wide range of farm buildings – barns, dairies, pigsties – that surrounded the house may also be provided. Recent developments were recorded: in 1607, the Chalfont St Giles (Buckinghamshire) incumbent had added two bays to the house – including a brewhouse – and had also planted a new orchard and built a cow house.

Incumbents had varied sources of income other than glebe lands and these were all recorded. It was particularly important to record tithing customs which, as will be seen in Chapter 6, were frequently the subject of dispute. Bishop Barrington asked for details of any 'Pensions, Augmentations, Gifts, or Bequests' made to the church and its ministers. He did not ask for details of fees charged for marriages, burials and mortuaries but other bishops frequently did.

Occasionally, terriers list church goods in the same way as inventories. In Barkham, Bray and Eastgarston (Berkshire), church houses are mentioned. Details of clerks' and sextons' wages and information on who was liable to repair churches and churchyard fences might also be provided. In the Quethiock (Cornwall) terrier of 1727, the legacy of Walter Coryton is recorded: he left £100 to the parish for the support of four unmarried women. Incumbents' obligations are sometimes mentioned. The vicar of Cumnor (Berkshire) was obliged to provide a 'drinking'.

Terriers declined in importance in the nineteenth century. The tithe legislation of 1836 removed the necessity of recording tithe customs. Most open fields had been enclosed; therefore the fear of encroachment on strips of glebe in the open fields was much reduced. However, the canon of 1603/4 remained in force until amended in the Convocation of 1891/2. Much greater emphasis was placed on the possessions of the church than on the sources of the incumbents' income. That remained the case throughout the twentieth century.

Terriers were compiled by churchwardens, the parish priest and perhaps other leading parishioners, all of whom signed their names (or made their marks). It is likely that they were scrutinized by the vestry. This certainly happened at St Mary's, Marlborough (Wiltshire) in 1698: the terrier states that it 'was read 17 Oct at a parish meeting and agreed to by all the parishioners then present'.

Published Glebe Terriers

BERKSHIRE
- Mortimer, Ian, ed. *Berkshire Glebe Terriers, 1634.* (Berkshire Record Society, 1995).

BUCKINGHAMSHIRE
- Reed, Michael, ed. *Buckinghamshire Glebe Terriers, 1578–1640.* (Buckinghamshire Record Society, 1997).

CORNWALL
- Potts, Richard, ed. *A Calendar of Cornish Glebe Terriers, 1673–1735.* (Devon & Cornwall Record Society, new series 19, 1974).

SHROPSHIRE
- *The Glebe Terriers of Shropshire.* (University of Keele Centre for Local History, 2002).

STAFFORDSHIRE
- Watts, Sylvia, ed. *Staffordshire Glebe Terriers 1585–1885.* (Collections for a History of Staffordshire, 4th series, 22–3, 2009).

WARWICKSHIRE
- Barratt, D.M., ed. *Ecclesiastical Terriers of Warwickshire Parishes.* 2 vols. (Dugdale Society 22 & 27, 1956–71).

WILTSHIRE
- Hobbs, Steve, ed. *Wiltshire Glebe Terriers 1588–1827.* (Wiltshire Record Society 56, 2003).

Easter Books

Easter offerings were an important component of parish priests' income. They are frequently mentioned in glebe terriers, which recorded amounts customarily paid; usually no more than 12 pence but perhaps graded according to status. This payment derived from the payment of personal tithes (see Chapter 7). Tradesmen were supposed to pay tithes based on their income, but, in a pre-literate era, without written accounts, their income was impossible to assess. Consequently, fixed payments made at Easter were substituted. Easter books and rolls – sometimes known as Paschal rolls – record amounts actually received. Usually every householder is listed, together with the amount paid. Sometimes, servants are also named. Other information may include notes on arrears and on their causes. Causes of non-payment may include poverty and nonconformity; in Ludlow (Shropshire), it is even possible to identify sufferers of the plague.

Easter books effectively serve as censuses of the population and are likely to be more accurate than most other population listings. If a run can be found, it may be possible to trace the movements of householders (and possibly servants) over several decades. They may also enable the social structure of parishes to be investigated. A full listing of those books known to survive is provided in the second part of:
- Wright, S.J. 'A Guide to Easter Books and Related Parish Listings', *Local Population Studies* 42, 1988, pp.18–31; 43, 1989, pp.13–27. www.localpopulationstudies.org.uk/backissues41-50.htm

Faculties

A faculty is a licence by a bishop or archdeacon authorizing the alteration, reconstruction or improvement of church fabric. Originally their scope was much wider. In the sixteenth century they were used, for example, to establish select vestries, to appropriate pews and to secure exemption from tithe. In the seventeenth and eighteenth centuries, they frequently relate to pews, galleries and burial vaults. The Victorians conducted much more extensive additions and restorations. In the twentieth century a faculty became necessary for the most minor changes but also for the erection of war memorials and the repair of war damage. Over 45 per cent of faculties in the Diocese of York 1613–1899 related to pews and seating.

Petitions for faculties provide details of the changes proposed and explain why they were needed. Frequently they are accompanied by detailed plans and elevations of the work proposed and sometimes of the structure being replaced, perhaps prepared by an architect or surveyor. The earliest surviving plan recorded in York Diocese is in the Archbishop's register, dated 1635; it relates to pews at Holmfirth (Yorkshire). There may also be extensive correspondence. The Intimation, or Proclamation Citatory, is the public announcement of the plans, read in church to allow for discussion and any objections to be made. Faculties issued may be recorded in the act books of Consistory courts. Comprehensive records of faculties can be found among diocesan records. Sometimes there is a separate faculty register. There may also be records of faculties among correspondence and other papers.

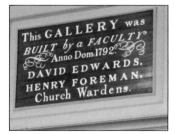

Faculties issued for particular parishes are likely to be found among parish records. The Heavitree

Memorial of a faculty at Lymington (Hampshire).

(Devon) parish records include faculties for the installation of a peal of eight bells to celebrate Queen Victoria's Golden Jubilee, for removal of galleries in 1924 and for installing a clock in the tower in 1910. The faculty issued for the restoration of the church at Stow (Lincolnshire) in 1865 gave extensive details of the proposed work and estimated the cost at £2,700, 'which sum has been raised by voluntary subscription', plus a further £500 to heighten the tower. The curate and churchwardens were authorized to carry the work 'into immediate effect', given that no opponents of the scheme had appeared to make their case.

Further Reading

The most substantial work on faculties is a listing of records in the Diocese of York:

- Evans, Peter. *Church Fabric in the York Diocese, 1613–1899: The Records of the Archbishops' Faculty Jurisdiction: A Handlist.* (Borthwick Texts & Calendars 19, 1995).

For church building plans (especially seating plans) among both faculty papers and parish records, see:

- Yates, Nigel. 'The Historical Value of Church Building Plans', *Archives* 18(78), 1987, pp.67–76.

For the nineteenth century, the database of plans from the Incorporated Church Building Society should also be mentioned:

- Church Plans Online
  www.churchplansonline.org

Seating Plans

'Take but degree away, untune that string,
And hark what discord follows!'

These words of Shakespeare provided the justification for a hierarchical society in early modern England. However, the evidence of disputes concerning pews suggests the opposite conclusion: the competition for status was at the root of much discord in parish churches over the right to sit in the most prestigious seats.

The social hierarchy was reflected in church. Gentlemen expected that parishioners would make way for their 'betters'. Many took a proprietorial attitude towards their pew, perhaps marking it with their name on a brass plate, or with their armorial bearings. In 1701, the Chichester (Sussex) accounts record 'that the seat or pew in the north east corner of the church of St Peter the lesse was built or made at the cost of John Oglander Esq., Nicholas Covert gent, and Katherine Tauke widowe, To whom only and to the temporary inhabitants of their respective now dwelling houses it doth belong to sit there.'

When new pews were erected in Rudgwick (Sussex) in 1846, farms assessed at more than £70 per year were allotted one pew, those worth over £35 merited half a pew and those worth between £20 and £35, just a third of a pew.

Some even used their wills to demand burial beneath their pew. On the other hand, English common law decreed that every resident of a parish had a right to a seat in the parish church.

The right to a seat was important. Everyone knew that they had a seat in church and thus in the community. Possession of a fixed seat engendered a feeling of community, enhanced worship, and helped to make the church the centre of that community.

A carved bench-end at Charlton Mackerell (Somerset).

The sexes generally sat separately in the fifteenth and sixteenth centuries; indeed, this was ordered by the 1549 prayer book. The Calstock (Cornwall) seating plan of 1587/8 shows that most did so. The Bishop of Norwich wrote to the churchwardens of West Walton (Norfolk) complaining that 'men and women do sit in the seats or stools ... promiscuously together, whereby there is no decency or order observed'. He directed that men should sit on the south side and women to the north but with 'an especial regard to the degrees and qualities of the persons so by you to be removed, displaced and placed, that there be not just cause of complaint'. He was hopeful!

Meanwhile, the poor were driven to the back of the church, and sometimes subjected to humiliating conditions. The vestry of St Edmund's, Salisbury in 1629 directed the poor to sit on 'fforms sett of purpose for them'; the words 'for the poore' were to be painted on them in 'great Red letters'. The churchwardens were to 'see who are missing, and to keepe backe that weekes pay vnles they can excuse it'.

Space was sometimes a problem. At Spelsbury (Oxfordshire), it was recorded that

> 'the churchwardens and the parishe have permitted Thomas Collinge, the younger, of Deane, and John Sansome of Spelsbury to set up a newe seate adjoyninge to the font, for their wives, under this condition that they shall avoide the seate as often as the fonte is used.'

Changes in status were reflected by changes in seating arrangements. The Lords Stourton lost their family pew when they sold the manor of Stourton (Wiltshire) in 1714, and were then allocated one in a much less prominent position.

The emphasis placed on hierarchy meant that seating arrangements were a perennial subject of dispute.[7] Jesus' injunction to 'take the lower seat' was much ignored. The churchwardens were faced with the invidious task of adjudicating between different claimants to particular pews. The introduction of pews meant that the free-for-all of an open church was replaced by an orderly system based on wealth, prestige and, sometimes, sex. However, the competition for seats was sometimes far from orderly.

As early as 1297, the Synod of Exeter had to assert the right of bishops to allocate seats. The bishops delegated the right to churchwardens but 'broyles about seates' became a, perhaps the, major source of litigation in the ecclesiastical courts.[8] The bishops were bombarded with complaints about seating, the church courts were full of litigation concerning pews and, worse, many people took matters into their own hands and caused disturbance during church services. At St Ebbs, Oxford 'this respondent offered to take her seate ... [when] the sayed Barbara iostled further into the seate & wolde not let her come into her own place there, wheupon this respondent sayed unto her, yf yowe will not let me come into mye owne seat I will sitt upon yor lappe ... and thereupon grewe further words of inconvenience betweene theme, as whore and basterd & such lyke.'[9]

Churchwardens' response to the possibility of such disputes was to make seating plans, showing where all members of the congregation would sit in church. Vestries were called upon to back them up. The earliest-known seating plan is for Trull (Somerset), dated 1569. In 1579, a 'booke' listing pews, their rental and their occupants was approved by the Stepney vestry. The vestry at Pittington (Co. Durham) agreed in 1584 that

'for the better hearing of divine servis, that everie house holder, as well gentle men as also husbandmen and cote men, shall taike suche place as is appointed for them ... paying for the same, for so many, roumes as everie man shall have, iiijd a roume at everie first entrye.'

This entry is followed by a listing of how seats were allocated, noting that some were built or repaired by the pew-holder himself.

Over two centuries later, in 1806 the vestry of Burton Bradstock (Dorset) resolved to take measures to prevent disputes and at the same time to improve the appearance of the pews. It ordered that

'the present Pews and Seats be all numbered and entered on the Church Book, expressing to whom they belong, and in what Right, at the expense of the Parish, and that all persons desirous of Painting their seats shall be at liberty to do so, provided they agree to follow a uniform and regular plan to be laid down by the Minister and Church Wardens.'

Seating plans were probably drawn up for most parishes. Many can still be found among parish records, or sometimes in diocesan archives. At Harford (Devon) a ledger contains a large number of such plans,

Numbered pew at Kenton (Devon).

recording changes in the allocation of pews over many decades. Such plans provide us with a virtual census of heads of households and an invaluable guide to social structure and status. They are particularly useful where men sat separately from women, since they then provide one of the few sources where women are likely to be named independently of their families. The local elite sat towards the front, under the pulpit; smallholders, servants and children sat behind them, with the poor at the back. Even in the 1860s, churchwardens were still being instructed 'to seat parishioners according to their order and degree'.[10] The most famous seating plan is undoubtedly that of Myddle (Shropshire), used by Richard Gough in the seventeenth century as the framework for his pioneering sociological study of the parish.[11]

Further Reading
Seating plans are discussed in:
- Thomas, Spencer. 'Pews: Their Setting, Symbolism and Significance', *Local Historian* 39(4), 2009, pp.267–86.

For a recent analysis of a seating plan, see:
- Pittman, Susan. 'The Social Structure and Parish Community of St Andrew's Church, Calstock, as Reconstituted from its Seating Plan c.1587/8', *Southern History* 20–21, 1998–99, pp.44–67.

Litigation
Clergymen and churchwardens owed obedience to bishops and archdeacons. Many appeared before episcopal and archidiaconal courts, either as witnesses, petitioners, or as the accused. The records of ecclesiastical courts are diocesan records; however, where a parish was concerned in a case, relevant papers were frequently deposited in parish chests. They may relate, for example, to presentments made by the churchwardens, to refusal to pay tithe or Easter offerings, or to penances imposed by the courts that had to be administered by the parish.

Such records were frequently copied into parish registers or account books. The parish registers of Sutton Valence (Kent) record: 'Nov 25th 1717. On which day Eliz Stace did public penance for ye foul sin of adultery committed with Tho: Hutchins junr in Sutton Vallence Church, as did Anney Hynds for ye foul sin of fornication committed with Tho: Daws.'

The Tavistock (Devon) parish records include articles against Jasper Cann, the vicar of the parish in 1682. It is evident that someone had a grudge against the vicar, as a wide range of accusations were flung at him. There had been a dispute between him and the churchwardens concerning expenses. On one occasion he was accused of refusing to conduct a communion service, 'for noe other reason as thou saydst because thou wouldst not weare a mended surplice & yt ye wyne prvided was unwholesome because not bought where thou wouldst have had it'.

The churchwardens' economizing had clearly upset the minister. His attitude clearly upset the churchwardens, who brought a variety of other charges, some of them implying sympathy with nonconformity; a serious charge under the Restoration regime. However, Cann remained vicar until 1690, even though it seems likely that the churchwardens threw every charge they could think of at him in an effort to be rid of a minister who challenged their stewardship.

The church courts did not have many teeth, especially in dealing with lay offenders. Mothers of illegitimate children could be required to do penance, as discussed in Chapter 3. Parish records frequently note the performance of this penalty. If the offender refused to do penance, the only remedy available to the court was excommunication. That was a serious matter, since it was intended to cut people off from society. A sentence found among the records of Luccombe (Somerset) dated 1628 commands the incumbent to denounce three parishioners and to 'admonish all Christian people by virtue hereof that they ... eschewe and avoide the society, fellowshippe and company of the said persons and neither eate nor drink, buy, sell or otherwise by any other manner of Means communicate with them, being members cut off from all Christian Society'. If they remained excommunicated, then the writ of 'De excommunicato Capiendo' could be directed to the sheriff, authorizing imprisonment.

Excommunicates could not be buried in parish churchyards: the register of Waterbeach (Cambridgeshire) for 1679 records 'Francis Wilson, excommunicated, buried in his orchard'. One wonders whether he was a Quaker. The growth of nonconformity after the Restoration meant the growth of contempt for the punishment of excommunication, thus rendering it nugatory. Quakers did not care where they were buried, although they – and other nonconformists – sometimes had their own burial grounds.

Contempt for the punishment also arose from its misuse. The churchwardens of Repton (Derbyshire) in 1595 were forced to pay 8 pence to 'Thomas Belcher of bryngyng a sertyfycatte for us being excommunycatt'. The next entry in their accounts probably explains why: no amount is given but the entry reads 'att Darby when we sartyfyed that our churche was glassed'. The bishop or archdeacon had presumably held them responsible for a gross dereliction of duty in not ensuring that their church was glazed, and imposed excommunication as the penalty.

Further Reading
The records of ecclesiastical courts are introduced in:
• Tarver, Anne. *Church Court Records: An Introduction for Family and Local Historians.* (Phillimore, 1995).

Registers of Services and Preachers
The parish priest has always been responsible for the conduct of services in the parish church, even if other ministers actually presided. Churchwardens' accounts, as we have seen, sometimes enable us to identify lecturers and preachers other than the incumbent. They may have thought that that was enough to comply with the 1603 canon requiring churchwardens to record 'the names of all Preachers which come to their church', in order that 'the bishop may understand … what Sermons are made'. Registers of preachers are rare before the late nineteenth century, although the names of 'strange preachers' may occasionally be found on odd pages of parish registers or churchwardens' accounts.

In the 1870s and 1880s, however, it became common for priests to keep registers of services and preachers. These give times and dates of all services conducted, the name of the celebrant and the size of his congregation. Sometimes they may include other memoranda. The service register of Huish Episcopi (Somerset), which dates from the 1840s, includes a list of sixty-three persons confirmed at Langport (Somerset) in 1852. The registers at St Martin's, Chichester (Sussex) date from 1878 and include extracts from Martha Dear's will. An exceptionally early register dating from 1828 belongs to St Mary's, Cheltenham; it includes details of collections taken in 1816–1836. Service registers continue to be kept to this day; if they have not been deposited in a record office, they may still be found in parish safes.

Forms of Prayer
Although the *Book of Common Prayer* provided the liturgy for routine worship in the church, special forms of prayer were issued for various occasions.[12] Payment for these may be recorded in churchwardens' accounts. Bedfordshire churchwardens' accounts record the purchase of prayers concerning the Turkish invasion of Hungary in 1566, the Cadiz expedition of 1586, the earthquake of 1586, and thanksgiving for the failure of the Babington Conspiracy in the same year, among others. The Meshaw (Devon) parish records include printed forms of prayer relating to the plague in 1720, freedom from disease in 1832 and the king's illness in 1830. Thanksgiving prayers were regularly issued: for example, Meshaw gave thanks for the victory over the Havannah in 1762 and for the birth of a prince in 1765.

Sermons

Occasionally, sermons are found among parish records. Frequently these are sermons preached by incumbents on various occasions in the history of the parish. For example, there is a bundle of twenty-four sermons preached by Rev Brocklebank at Longbridge Deverill (Wiltshire) during the First World War. In the same county, some nineteenth-century sermons of the Littlewood family at Edington were printed and placed in the parish chest. At a much earlier date, the diatribe of Rev Strong concerning poor relief at Layston (Hertfordshire) in 1636 is still among the parish records.

Church Magazines

In the late nineteenth century, many energetic incumbents launched church magazines, usually published monthly. These contained a wide range of material: local and national news, letters from the incumbent and bishop, notices of forthcoming events, reports of meetings, obituaries, baptism, marriage and burial announcements, advertisements, the names of those responsible for various duties such as flower-arranging, visiting, youth clubs, prayer groups, etc. Sometimes they were issued in conjunction with diocesan magazines. They still are: such magazines continue to be published to this day. Runs and individual copies can frequently be found among parish records, although it is rare to find a complete set of magazines. They are invaluable sources regarding the life of the church at the time they were issued and provide much information on who was doing what.

Churchyard Fencing

It has already been noted that terriers frequently record the obligation of parishioners to repair churchyard fencing. This obligation was frequently imposed on the occupiers of land. At Cowfold (Sussex), no fewer than eighty-one tenants shared this obligation in 1631. The initials of those responsible are deeply incised on the fence itself. Lists of those required to make repairs were made, either on separate sheets or written into accounts and other books. Broomfield (Essex) has a sequence of churchyard fence lists, 1569 to 1834, identifying the properties responsible for repair. Of course, those obligated to undertake repairs did not always do so and there are many presentments for their failures. Four men at Sutton (Worcestershire) were presented in 1621 'for not making of the church wall, which lies downe to the ground, and bodyes of the dead are dayly ready to be digged up of hogges'.

Chapter 6

PARISH REGISTERS OF BAPTISMS, MARRIAGES AND BURIALS

The year revolves, and I again explore
The simple annals of my parish poor
What infant-members in my flock appear
What pairs I bless'd in the departed year
And who, of old or young, or nymphs or swains
Are lost to life, its pleasures and its pains
George Crabbe, *The Parish Register*

Parish registers of baptisms, marriages and burials were the commonest records in parish chests. Consequently, the term 'parish records' is frequently used – wrongly – as a synonym for parish registers. There are, as this book demonstrates, a wide variety of parish records other than parish registers. Nevertheless, baptisms, marriages and burials are of great importance to both family and local historians, and these registers attract more attention from them than any of the other documents from parish chests.

Much attention has also been paid to them by the writers of handbooks and manuals, including the present author. One of the aims here is to draw attention to the wide variety of other parish records that are available. The temptation to re-invent the wheel will therefore not be taken here. For detailed accounts of parish registers, the researcher should consult the books listed at the end of this chapter. Here, only a brief summary will be offered.

Thomas Cromwell, Henry VIII's vicegerent, ordered parish priests to keep registers of baptisms, marriages and burials in 1538. The order has never been rescinded, and parish registers continue to be maintained by Anglican clergy to this day, despite the advent of civil registration. It was the duty of the churchwardens, every Sunday, to ensure that 'the minister enter therein all christnings, weddings, and burials that have been the week before; and at the bottom of every page, they shall (with the minister) subscribe their names'.[1] Cromwell's stated intention was to provide a record that would show who was entitled to inherit property and to 'avoid dispute touching ages, titles, or lineal descents'. The register was described by Burn as 'good evidence' and 'the falsifying it is punishable at the common law'.[2] Many feared that Cromwell also intended to use the registers to impose taxation. It is not clear whether that was in fact the intention; however, if it was, he decided that, in the wake of the Pilgrimage of Grace, the danger of rebellion against such a tax was too great. Nevertheless, duties were imposed on baptisms, marriages and burials on two subsequent occasions: between 1694 and 1705, and between 1783 and 1794. Both were unsuccessful; so much so that after the repeal of 1794, clergy who had failed to collect the duty had to be indemnified by Act of Parliament.

Many babies were baptized in this font at Kenton (Devon).

In the earliest registers no set format of entry was laid down. The entries of baptisms, marriages and burials were intermingled. Latin was frequently used. This should present no problems to the non-Latinist, since the Latin terms used were common form; the meaning of words such as 'baptismata', 'matrimonia' and 'sepultura' are fairly obvious. Some registers provided much detail, especially when a vital event concerned the local gentry or the clergy. When the daughter of the county sheriff was baptized at Repton (Derbyshire) in 1620, the entry read: 'Elizabeth ye daughter of Mr Godfrey Thacquer esquire this yeare sheriff and of Jane his wife was baptised ye 23 of March.' Baptismal entries usually – but not always – record the names of both parents.

Marriage entries generally give the names of both partners, sometimes recording the parishes they came from and their occupations, although minimal information might also be given. The register of St Bridget's, Chester, states that 'William Washington wedded 5 Feb 1560'. By contrast, the register of Bolton le Sands (Lancashire) records 'Crestafor Caton of Garstange black smith & Dorythy Manser of the parish of Melling licenced by Mr Barowes 2 July' were married on 3 August 1667.

Burial entries can also be very brief, but that is not always the case: the Repton (Derbyshire) register records that 'Mr William Ullock the Head-schoolemaster of Repton-schoole died May the 13° and was buried in the Chancell.' Sometimes unusual detail is recorded. The Glasbury (Breconshire) burial register records 'Three children born att a Birth to Lowry, the wife of Tho Wm Lewes, buried Octob 1664.' Occasionally, no name is given: in 1584, the Chippenham (Wiltshire) register records the burial of 'a stranger died in Mr Robert Franklyns barne'. The incumbent and the churchwardens usually signed the registers at the end of each year.

Sixteenth-century parish registers were mostly compiled in paper books. Relatively few now survive. Most of those that do are copies made in compliance with canons issued in 1598 and 1604. These required the registers to be kept in parchment books for their better preservation. The old registers had to be copied. The churchwardens of St Matthew, Friday Street (London) purchased 'a booke of parchment ruled containyng 97 leaues' for this purpose, and paid out 30 shillings to have their old register copied into it. The latter would then have been discarded. The likelihood is that only the essentials were copied; much information that would have been of interest to researchers has probably been lost. The fact that the same clergyman and churchwardens signed the entries for every year in a sixteenth-century register does not mean that they held office for more than half a century; rather, it means that they complied with the canons of 1598 and 1604.

These canons also required churchwardens to send a transcript of register entries to the bishop every year. This extended a practice that had already existed in the Diocese of Canterbury and the Archdeaconry of Lincoln. In most dioceses, some bishops' transcripts (BTs) survive from the adoption of the canons until the early nineteenth century, except for the period of the civil war and Interregnum (1640–60). The churchwardens of Reading (Berkshire) in 1624–5 recorded the payment of 5 shillings 'for writing the Regester in parchment and sending it to salsburie'. Survival is, however, patchy and there are none at all for Essex prior to 1800.

The mid-seventeenth-century civil war resulted in the loss of many parish registers and a revolutionary (but temporary) change in the way that they were compiled. In 1653 Parliament removed their keeping from the hands of the clergy and entrusted them to a lay officer confusingly known as a 'parish register'. Appointments to the position were frequently noticed in the register: at Repton (Derbyshire) on 31 December 1655, it was recorded that 'Geo: Roades ye day and yeare above written approved and sworne Register for ye parish of Repton in ye County of Derby By me James Abney'.

Under this Act, marriage became a civil matter conducted before Justices of the Peace. Hitherto, banns had been called but had rarely been recorded. The 1653 Act required banns to be called three times and recorded in the register. A typical 1653 entry reads:

'Evan Pritchard and Judith Fleming both of our parish of Giles Cripplegate were published three several market dayes in Newgate Market in three several weekes concerning theire intention of marriage viz – on the 1st, 5th, and 12th days of October 1653 and married the 23rd day of the said month. Per Justice Blomer.'

The office of 'parish register', and the practice of civil marriage, did not last long. When Charles II was restored to the throne in 1660, the legislation of Interregnum Parliaments was declared invalid and the keeping of parish registers was restored to the parochial clergy. It was not until 1834 that civil marriage was reintroduced.

Shortly after the Restoration, in 1666, Parliament enacted that all corpses should be buried in a woollen shroud, and from 1678 a fine of £5 was imposed for any failure to comply with the law. Parishes were required to keep affidavits showing compliance with the law. The law was frequently evaded, but, if affidavits survive, useful information may be found in them: for example, the affidavit for the burial of Hannah Friend at Cowden (Kent) in 1679 reveals that both her husband and her son were named Robert. Two witnesses were also named. Affidavits ceased to be legally required after 1814.

The history of parish registers has to be seen against the background of marriage law and customs. It is too frequently assumed that marriage in England has always meant marriage in a church. That is not correct. In common law, a valid marriage was simply an agreement made between the couple in the presence of witnesses and did not require the presence of a priest. It was only in the later medieval period that marriage by a priest at the church door (not the altar) became customary. Canon law required couples to either have banns called, or to obtain a marriage licence, before marriage could take place. In the early eighteenth-century register of Stratton (Cornwall), the register regularly records whether marriages were by banns or by licence.

Couples increasingly sought to evade the necessity of banns or licence, given that they could have a perfectly valid common-law marriage without them. The bishops could prevent the clergy under their jurisdiction from presiding over 'irregular' marriage but they could not prevent those clergy who were not under their jurisdiction from doing so. There were many

Limpley Stoke (Wiltshire) church porch. Weddings took place in the porch in earlier centuries.

places outside of episcopal jurisdiction; the Liberty of the Fleet Prison was particularly notorious in this respect. In the mid-eighteenth century perhaps half of all London marriages were irregular.

It was against this background that Hardwicke's Marriage Act was passed in 1753. It eliminated the possibility that marriage could take place without banns or licence. Marriages valid in English law henceforth had to be conducted by an Anglican clergyman in the home parish of one of the parties. Only Jews and Quakers were exempt from this rule. The Act also introduced the use of printed books of forms for the recording of both marriages and banns. This ensured that marriage registers would be kept much more carefully than had hitherto been the case.

The advantages of using forms to compile registers rapidly became obvious. With effect from 1 January 1813, they were used for baptism and burial registers as well. These registers became much easier for researchers to use.

Unfortunately, however, parish registers were ceasing to be comprehensive in the early nineteenth century. In particular, many baptisms were not being recorded. Nonconformists did not bring their babies to be baptized in Anglican churches. Almost as many churchgoers attended nonconformist churches as attended their own parish churches, as was subsequently demonstrated by the 1851 religious census. Furthermore, attendance at church was decreasing, especially in the major cities. Admittedly, many who did not regularly attend the Church of England did have church weddings, and also brought their children for baptism. Nevertheless, the parochial registration system was increasingly unfit for purpose. That purpose remained, in the eyes of the authorities, to provide adequate proof of title in a society where inheritance determined the ownership of land. It was not nonconformist complaints, loud as they were, that led to the introduction of civil registration in 1837. Rather, it was the fact that the parochial registration system could not always provide proof of descent for the purposes of inheritance law.

The 1836 Act was a typically British compromise. The church obviously had a vested interest in retaining control over marriage. Consequently, the reform allowed its clergy to continue recording marriages in its parish registers. Henceforward, however, duplicate registers were required. Each parish was issued with two separate books of forms to be filled in. One copy was to be retained by the parish; the other was to be sent to the district registrar when completed (a very few, even now, have still not been completed and are therefore still held by parishes). The incumbent was to make quarterly returns of marriages to the Registrar General. However, the monopoly of the Church of England over legal marriages was ended. The

Act permitted the marriages of nonconformists and Roman Catholics to be conducted by their own clergy, in the presence of a registrar. Registrars could also conduct civil marriages themselves.

The Act had no effect on the keeping of parochial baptism and burial registers, which continue to be kept by the clergy to this day. However, district registrars were required to keep separate registers of births and deaths. Parish registers may sometimes be more informative than the civil registers and genealogists should always bear them in mind when using the latter, especially in view of the fact that many have been deposited in record offices, where they can be consulted directly. The civil registers are not open to public inspection. In order to consult them, it is necessary to obtain certificates of births, marriages and deaths. However, since 1837 there has been a dramatic decline in church attendance and an increasing use of non-parochial cemeteries. Consequently, the proportion of vital events recorded in parish registers has been substantially reduced.

Recent and current parish registers are still held in parish safes. Incumbents are only expected to deposit registers whose oldest entry is 150 years old or whose final entry is over 100 years old.

As already noted, there was no specific format for parish register entries before 1753. The printed forms for registering marriages introduced under Hardwicke's Act of that year included columns for the names and parishes of the parties, the date and place of marriage, whether by banns or licence, whether with the consent of parents or guardians, the name of the officiating minister and the signatures of parties, witnesses and minister. The forms used from 1837 also included columns for indicating ages and occupations, although the former was frequently given as either 'minor' or 'of full age'.

After 1812, the printed forms used for registering baptisms included columns for recording the date of baptism, the Christian name of the child, the names, abode and 'quality, trade or profession' of the parents, and the name of the officiating clergyman. The forms used for burial registers had columns for recording name, abode, place of burial, age, and the name of the clergyman who presided. There were unfortunately no columns for occupations or for the names of the parents of deceased children.

Two other sources are closely associated with parish registers. Transcripts of them were made annually and sent into the Diocesan Registry. These bishops' transcripts are not parish records and are therefore not considered in detail here. Marriage licences were presented by the parties to the celebrant and usually destroyed; on very rare occasions they were preserved and can still be found among parish records. It is, however, likely to be more productive to search for records of the issuing of marriage licences among diocesan archives. The holdings of surviving bishops' transcripts and marriage licence records are summarily listed in Jeremy Gibson's *Bishops' Transcripts and Marriage Licences, Bonds and Allegations: A Guide to their Location and Indexes* (6th ed. Family History Partnership, 2013).

Most original parish registers have been deposited in local record offices. A summary listing is provided in Cecil Humphery-Smith's *Phillimore's Atlas and Index of Parish Registers* (3rd ed. Phillimore & Co., 2003). Comprehensive listings of original registers, bishops' transcripts and other copies can be found in the county volumes of the Society of Genealogists' *National Index of Parish Registers* series. Many transcripts are available online; these include many printed editions of registers that have been digitized. Over 1,400 marriage registers were printed in Phillimore's parish registers series. The Parish Register Society published over 100 registers, and there are or have been separate societies publishing parish registers in many counties; the societies for Lancashire, Shropshire, Staffordshire and Yorkshire have been particularly prolific. The Harleian Society has published eighty-nine registers, mainly for London. Many family history societies have published parish registers: for details, see the publication pages on their websites (listed at www.genuki.org.uk/Societies). Most published parish registers are held by the Society of Genealogists, as are many unpublished transcripts. For details, search at www.sog.org.uk/the-library.

Increasingly, original registers are being digitized and made available on the internet. Many registers from Cheshire, Cornwall, Derbyshire, Essex, Kent and other counties are freely available at Family Search www.familysearch.org/search (scroll down and click 'United Kingdom & Ireland' for a detailed list). Registers from North-West Kent are available at the Medway Ark http://cityark.medway.gov.uk. Registers held by London Metropolitan Archives are available on a pay-per-view database at Ancestry www.ancestry.co.uk/uklma. A variety of other parish registers have been digitized at www.findmypast.co.uk. No doubt by the time you read this, many more will be available online.

There are also numerous indexes online. The most important of these is the *International Genealogical Index*, popularly known as the *IGI* www.familysearch.org/search/collection/igi. This only covers baptisms and marriages; for burials, wide coverage is provided by the *National Burial Index* www.ffhs.org.uk/projects/nbi. These are the most comprehensive indexes available but their coverage is far from being complete. Other major indexes include *Boyd's Marriage Index* www.findmypast.co.uk with some 7,000,000 entries; *Pallot's Index 1780–1837* http://search.ancestry.co.uk/search/db. aspx?dbid=5967 which is particularly strong on the City of London, although it also includes parishes in most counties; and the *Joiner Marriage*

Index http://joinermarriageindex.co.uk covering much of the north of England. Boyd's index is available free to members of the Society of Genealogists at www.sog.org.uk. Numerous online and offline marriage indexes are listed by Jeremy Gibson, Elizabeth Hampson and the present author in *Marriage Indexes for Family Historians* (9th ed., Family History Partnership, 2009).

It is important to appreciate that these indexes are just that: indexes. They are intended to enable you to locate entries in original parish registers. They do not necessarily provide you with all the information to be found in those entries. For example, occupations and ages may be given in the original but not in the index. It is always important to check original documents rather than just relying on the index. The *IGI* is particularly helpful in this respect, since it indexes microfilmed documents that can be borrowed through the Family History Libraries of the Church of Jesus Christ of Latter Day Saints. However, when consulting these documents, it is important to check their status; they could be microfilms of printed or manuscript copies rather than of the original registers. The evidential value of the original register is always to be preferred. If a digitized version of the original register can be found, that is much to be preferred to any transcript. It should provide you with an exact reproduction, although even the photographer can miss the odd page!

Sadly, of course, many parish registers have been lost. Sometimes the details contained in lost registers can be found in the bishops' transcripts or in the records of marriage licences. Bear in mind, too, that burials may be recorded in churchwardens' accounts.

Further Reading
Much more information on parish registers is given in:
• Raymond, Stuart A. *Parish Registers: A History and Guide.* (Family History Partnership, 2009).
The classic history of parish registers, now rather out of date but still useful, is:
• Steel, D.J. *National Index of Parish Registers: Volume 1, Sources of Births, Marriages and Deaths before 1837 (1).* (Society of Genealogists, 1968).
Both of these volumes include references to many other works.

Chapter 7

TITHE RECORDS

Come, ponder well, for 'tis no jest,
To laugh it would be wrong,
The troubles of a worthy priest,
The burden of my song.

This priest he merry is and blithe,
Three quarters of the year,
But oh! It cuts him like a scythe
When tithing time draws near.

He then is full of frights and fears
As one at point to die,
And long before the day appears
He heaves up many a sigh.

For then the farmers come, jog, jog,
Along the miry road,
Each heart as heavy as a log,
To make their payment good.

In sooth the sorrow of such days,
Is not to be expressed,
When he that takes and he that pays,
Are both alike distressed.

Now all unwelcome at his gates,
The clumsy swains alight,
With rueful faces and bald pates:
He trembles at the sight.

And well he may, for well he knows,
Each bumpkin of the clan,
Instead of paying what he owes,
Will cheat him if he can.

One talks of mildew and of frost
And one of storms and hail,
And one of pigs that he has lost,
By maggots at the tail.

Oh, why were farmers made so coarse,
Or clergy made so fine?
A kick that scarce would move a horse,
May kill a sound divine.

The Yearly Distress, or, Tithing-Time at Stock in Essex,
William Cowper

Tithing, that is, giving a tenth of one's income to God, is a biblical principle. In Genesis 28:22, Jacob promised the Lord that 'of all that you give me I will give you a tenth'. The Anglo-Saxons went back to the Old Testament when they instituted the payment of tithe. Tithing underpinned the development of the parochial system, as was seen in Chapter 2. The church successfully maintained its right to tithe for a millennium. The official attitude was summed up by John Myrc in his *Instructions for Parish Priests:*[1]

Every mon hys teythynge schale paye
Both of smale and of grete
Of schep and swyn & other nete
Tythe of huye [hay] and of honed [hand labour]
Goth by costome of the londe.

The principle of tithing was widely accepted in the medieval period. Non-payment was regarded as a mortal sin, despite the fact that it was a regressive tax and frequently arbitrary. Tithing attracted little open opposition until the Quakers refused to pay in the late seventeenth century. Nevertheless, evasion was widespread and many testators acknowledged their 'tithes forgot' in their wills. For priests, pastoral duties conflicted with their legal entitlement. As Chaucer put it, the parish priest was 'Ful loth … to cursen for his tithes'. Tithes could set parson against parishioner, poisoning the relationship between them. Tithe was uncertain in its incidence, subject to considerable fluctuation and required regular (contentious) revaluations to ensure fairness.[2] There were a host of local peculiarities, with virtually every parish operating a different system. The courts could sanction both gross oppressiveness from tithe owners and flagrant evasion by tithe payers.

Substantial tithe barns, such as this one at Bradford on Avon (Wiltshire), were sometimes required to store tithe.

By the eighteenth century, tithe was paid almost entirely by farmers. It was a tax on yield, and bore more heavily on labour-intensive arable than on pastoral farmers, especially on improved land. It was far from being a fair way of financing the church and, not surprisingly, opposition to tithe came primarily from farmers. Unfortunately for tithe owners, the farmers knew how to defend themselves against what they saw as the rapacity of the clergy. They preferred litigation to affray and lawyers made fortunes from tithe disputes.

Theoretically, tithes were of three types. Praedial tithes were levied on the produce of the ground, such as grain and hay. Mixed tithes were due on produce nourished by the ground: cattle, milk, sheep, etc. Tithes on the produce of man's labour were personal tithes, first demanded by the Fourth Lateran Council of 1215.

Institutional rectors, and absentees, sometimes made an alternative division. The great tithes of corn, grain, hay and wood might be paid to the rector; the small tithes, covering everything else, to the vicar. Such a division was not, however, invariable: in Staffordshire, for example, the tithe of hay frequently went to the vicar.

Tithes could be exacted on most sources of income: crops, livestock, fisheries, minerals, timber, salt, rents and even on servants' wages. In Warwickshire hops, cabbages and fish were among the more unusual tithable items mentioned in terriers. They could not, however, be levied on mineral extractions: in Wednesbury (Staffordshire) it was stated in 1730 that 'There is a very great coal mine in the parish which is prejudicial to the vicar by destroying a great deal of the ground otherwise profitable to him.' Unfortunately, although the original miners were prepared to pay compensation, the Quakers who took it over from them did not pay tithe on principle. They had no legal obligation towards the vicar.

Tithes were originally payable in kind. The tithe owner collected the tenth sheaf of corn, the tenth cow, the tenth pig, even the tenth pail of milk, when the tithe payer indicated that the produce was ready for collection. It was relatively straightforward to collect the tenth stook of corn. It was, however, much more difficult to collect the tenth pail of milk and not always worth the expense of doing so. Should it be collected by the parson or delivered by his parishioner? Collecting personal tithes was even more difficult: how could one work out what a tradesman should pay, when he did not keep accounts? The difficulties involved in collecting tithes were considerable, sometimes insuperable, and not only for the tithe owner. The tithe payer would have to wait for the tithe owner before he could remove his crop from the field. If the latter delayed his appearance and the weather was bad, the crop could easily be damaged. However, the tithe owner could not visit all his parishioners at once.

These difficulties led many incumbents to accept payment by modus; that is, a customary monetary payment in lieu of tithes. Agreements could be made to pay a specific sum in lieu of tithes on particular produce, perhaps 2 pence for a swarm of bees. Alternatively, agreements could be made to commute all tithes for a set payment. The danger was inflation. A modus, once established, easily became accepted as custom and the value of payments could decline as inflation increased. In the eighteenth century, moduses agreed centuries earlier had sometimes become ridiculous; ½d for a calf was scarcely worth collecting. It was better to accept a composition to be agreed every year, which could be altered to take changing values into account. When disputes broke out, clergy who could not agree with parishioners on a reasonable monetary payment frequently insisted on payment in kind, creating much resentment. A correspondent to the *Monthly Magazine* in 1798 drew the obvious conclusion: 'Very few clergymen in England who take tithes in kind retain the good opinion of their parishioners and therefore have but little prospect of ministering to their religious improvement.'

Disputes were particularly common when a new clergyman arrived. His parishioners had plenty of experience of the local system; he had none. He needed to have his wits about him. It helped if his predecessors had ensured that the customs of the parish, and any agreements they had made with tithe payers, were written down. Hence the importance of the glebe terrier. It also helped if predecessors had not allowed a fixed modus to become customary. John Reynolds of Thorley's advice to his successor was sound:

> 'as the roads are bad for carrying off the Tith corn, I advise my successors rather to compound than take it in kind ... this one thing I only beg of them, not to accept of just the same summe for which I have compounded with them, lest they should in time bring it into a modus.'

The process of commutation probably began with personal tithe. It was difficult to assess the tithable income of tradesmen in towns. It could not be easily measured, especially given that many were illiterate and incapable of keeping accounts. In 1228, Bishop Niger ordered that London's tithes should be based on the rental value of property, and the idea was adopted in other boroughs. Disputes, however, continued. In the sixteenth century, Archbishop Cranmer had to intervene and, eventually, a statute was passed in 1546 confirming London tithes at 2s 9d for every pound of rental value.[3] Yet still disputes continued! The full amount due was rarely collected. It has been calculated that over a third of city incumbents took action in the church courts to recover tithes that had been withheld.[4]

The enclosure movement (see Chapter 8) offered a way out for those rectors fortunate to live in open field parishes. The object of enclosure was primarily agricultural improvement, but both clergy and landowners were usually agreed on the need to commute tithes. Frequently, land was allotted to the incumbent in substitution for his right to tithe. Some 70 per cent of Enclosure Acts passed between 1757 and 1835 included provision for tithe commutation.[5] As noted in Chapter 2, such commutation played an important role in improving the status of clergymen and in the rise of the clergy as a profession for gentlemen. The attitude of the yeomen of Launton (Oxfordshire) was commented on by their incumbent: 'Reverence for my office they had none; consideration for me as a gentleman and landlord and occupant of a large glebe, they had.'[6]

Tithes were contentious. It was not always clear whether they were due to the vicar or the lay impropriator. Conversion of arable land to pasture might increase the value of the small tithes due to the vicar and decrease the value of the great tithes due to the rector. There was much dispute between the two. The lay impropriator of a rectory was likely to be much more aggressive and grasping than the clergy: tithes to him were a business arrangement and nothing to do with religion. Other problems related to new crops, such as hops and potatoes, which did not always fit easily into the system. Also was a turkey a domestic fowl or a wild bird? Then there were the perennial problems involved in collecting tithes of milk, honey, hemp, flax, and garden produce.

Issues such as these clogged up the ecclesiastical courts and would have done so even more if clergy had been in a better position to take tithe payers to court. The vicar of Pittington (Co. Durham) was not alone when he noted that 'I was obliged to sit down and suffer wrong, because I had no Fortune to suffer a trial at law.'

It has been calculated that over half of Wiltshire parishes experienced at least one tithe dispute between 1660 and 1740.[7] In the Diocese of Lichfield there were over 550 tithe cases between 1690 and 1830.[8] Even before then, in 1550, the Bishop of Salisbury had instructed his clergy that

'Forasmuche as by Reason of the great diuersite of customes vsed in … paing tythes offringes & other ecclesiasticall dutes muche sute in the law, myche contaversye & dissencion dothe daylie arise & increase more & more, the said customes beinge so dyuerse & so variable that skarse ij parishes be lycke in all pointes thruglie; therfor my lorde Requireth that a byll be made of all the customes obserued in yor parishes consernyng the prmises by thadvyse of the parson, vicarr, or curatt & the church wardens of the parishe.'[9]

This directive was unique in its time, but its intent was subsequently carried out by recording details of tithing customs in glebe terriers.

Tithes gave rise to the accumulation of a great mass of paper. Mention has already been made of ecclesiastical court records and glebe terriers. Occasionally details of a court case will be recorded among parish records. Tithing customs and agreements were frequently written in parish registers or churchwardens' accounts. The earliest churchwardens' accounts from Badsey (Worcestershire) commence in 1525 with an agreement 'ffor tythyng of shepe': 'Yf the shepe remeyne from myndsomer or wt in one monyth aft yt then at the nexth sheryng he shall pay all hys tyhth.'

Some clergy kept accounts books recording tithes received. The Datchworth (Hertfordshire) tithe accounts record the names of tithe payers and the amounts paid. The rector's expenses in collecting tithes are also noted, his 'tything men' and other servants are named, and income from the sale of tithe produce is recorded. Wymondham (Norfolk) has a unique collection of tithe books, extending from 1640 through to 1836, and its parish records include numerous papers relating to tithe disputes. Fressingfield (Suffolk) has an even longer run of tithe books, extending (with breaks) from 1567 to 1779.

Tithe books give us a great deal of varied information. Some include terriers of particular farms, notes on occupations and population, religious affiliations and personal observations. The characters of some Kirstead (Norfolk) inhabitants are described in its 1753 tithe book; for example, 'a singularly silly designing Knave' and 'an honest good-natured woman'.[10]

The Daventry (Northamptonshire) tithe book includes various eighteenth-century lists of farmers in the parish, showing the amount of tithe payable and sometimes their yard lands. This volume records a convoluted dispute between the perpetual curate of Daventry and the tenants of the rectorial estate, eventually settled when Christ College Oxford, as lay owners of the rectory, required its tenants to pay small tithes to the curate. The latter recorded that:

> 'I have rescued sixteen yard land from the power of an oppressor and made them tytheable as well as other parts of the field … So that now the minister has a right to all the small tythes that arise in the parish and no body starts any pretended privilege or exemption.'

Many similar records can be found among parish records. The most important tithe records, however, are the maps and apportionments of the early nineteenth century. Since the seventeenth century, agricultural propagandists had argued for a general commutation of tithe. Board of Agriculture reports, published between 1793 and 1814, were almost unanimous in attributing most of the difficulties faced by agricultural improvers to the existence of tithe. Adam Smith described them as 'an effectual bar' to agricultural improvement.[11]

The Tithe Commutation Act of 1836 was the culmination of centuries of protest against tithes. It substituted corn rents, that is, monetary payments linked to the price of corn, for the payment of tithes in kind. Initially, the clergy benefited from a more realistic assessment of the value of tithes. The Tithe Commissioners took into account small tithes, hitherto not worth collecting; they disallowed outdated moduses, and assessed crops that had not previously been tithable. In Staffordshire, tithe owners' income was increased – sometimes considerably – in over 50 per cent of awards.[12] The landed interest acquiesced, content that the tithe question was finally to be put to rest.

The Tithe Commissioners divided up the country into 14,829 tithe districts; mostly parishes, although in large parishes further division into a number of districts was occasionally necessary. Next, they investigated the extent to which commutation had already taken place. If tithes had been commuted by enclosure, no further action was necessary. The results of their inquiries can be found in the tithe files, now in The National Archives, class IR18. These are not parish records.

The third stage in the process was to reach an agreement between tithe owners and landowners, or to impose an award. The actual value of tithes, including those that had never been collected, had to be established by valuers. This notional rent charge was then apportioned between the landowners, preferably with their agreement. If they could not agree, the commissioners made an impartial award. The amount assessed formed the basis from which the amount payable each year was calculated; it varied depending upon the price of corn.

Details of the agreement or award were recorded in a tithe apportionment and map. These cover some 75 per cent of England and Wales. Three copies of each were compiled. One was retained by the Tithe Commissioners and is now in The National Archives (apportionments in IR29, maps in IR30). Another copy was deposited in the Diocesan Registry, and the third in the parish chest. The diocesan and parish copies are now normally in local record offices. Occasionally, copies were also made for the private use of local landowners and may be found among their estate archives (often in local record offices). Maps and apportionments are frequently very bulky.

Tithe apportionments show how the overall rent charge for the district was divided among individual landowners. They usually follow a standard column format. A preamble indicates whether the document is an award or an agreement, giving statistics as to the area covered and its state of cultivation, with details of any tithe commutations or exemptions. Schedules record names of all landowners and occupiers, giving a numbered description of each tithe area, noting its acreage, name and state of cultivation, and assessing rent charge. Apportionments close with a summary of the schedule, listing landowners alphabetically, naming their tenants and stating the total rent charge for their holdings. They are highly accurate, apart from acreages (see below). Accuracy was essential, in view of the fact that money and property were concerned.

Accompanying tithe maps were much less uniform, although all tithe areas were numbered, facilitating comparison with apportionments. Landowners were reluctant to pay for a full survey, so maps vary greatly in scale and accuracy. Only a small proportion received the commissioners' seal of approval, which was required for them to be regarded as legal evidence. Reliance cannot be placed upon acreages stated in unsealed tithe maps and their accompanying apportionments.

The map and the apportionment were not necessarily compiled at the same time. There could be a delay of a few years after the map was drawn before the apportionment was made. Most tithe districts were mapped by 1850; a few, however, took much longer and the last map was not compiled until 1883. Altered apportionments were made when changes to the landscape, such as the construction of a railway, affected the rent charge. These are filed with the original apportionments in The National Archives. Parish records sometimes include certificates of redemption of tithe rent charges.

The tithe surveys enable us to identify our ancestors' land holdings. Details given in apportionments can usefully be compared with the census returns of 1841 and 1851, together with any rate assessments that may survive among parish records and with a variety of other sources. The maps form the basis from which we can trace the development of the landscape over many previous centuries.

Tithe maps were the first large-scale mapping survey of England and Wales and the first systematic national survey of land use. The maps show the layout of fields, roads, buildings and other landscape features. Apportionments provide statistics showing the state of cultivation of the fields, the area covered by roads, commons and wastes, and the extent of any lands exempt from tithe. The categories used, however, are very generalized and over-simplified; moreover, surveys were compiled over a period of time so a full survey does not necessarily reflect land use on a specific date. They do, however, enable us to link particular crops to particular fields. Very few other historical documents provide similar information. The tithe surveys may provide the only information available to reconstruct land use and farming patterns. Maps are likely to show houses and other buildings such as churches, inns, schools and factories. The names of their owners and occupiers can be identified from apportionments.

Maps provide definitive statements of parish and township boundaries, which had usually been unchanged for many centuries. Sometimes disputes over boundaries had to be resolved by the assistant commissioners and the tithe files may provide useful information on such disputes.

Field boundaries are also mapped; consequently it is possible to identify such remnants of open fields as survived. The field names recorded provide valuable evidence, not only for studying place names but also for agricultural and landscape historians. They are frequently unrecorded elsewhere. Villages and hamlets are depicted in the final stages of their evolution as solely agricultural settlements. Roads and rights of way are depicted as they were before the internal combustion engine and as they had mostly been (apart from the turnpikes) for centuries. The early stages of industrialization are also depicted.

If tithes had already been commuted by enclosure, or extinguished as a result of former ecclesiastical ownership of the land, there was no need for a tithe map and apportionment. Occasionally, if all the tithes had not been commuted at enclosure, both enclosure map and tithe map, together with their awards or apportionments, may be available. Parishes enclosed after the 1836 Act may also have both maps.

A variety of other tithe documents created by the Tithe Commissioners are held by The National Archives and described in its leaflet 'Tithes' at www.nationalarchives.gov.uk/records/research-guides/tithe-records.htm. These are not parish records and are therefore outside the scope of this book.

Tithe records form a basic source for a wide range of research into social, economic and religious history. The surveys form a starting-point for historical research in parishes where they were compiled.

Further Reading
A detailed account of the tithe problem in the eighteenth and nineteenth centuries is provided by:
- Evans, Eric J. *The Contentious Tithe: The Tithe Problem and English Agriculture, 1750–1850.* (Routledge & Kegan Paul, 1976).

For a brief introduction to pre-1836 tithe books, see:
- Evans, Nesta. 'Tithe Books as a Source for the Local Historian', *Local Historian* 14, 1980, pp.24–7.

The authoritative guide to tithe maps and apportionments is:
- Kain, Roger J.P., & Prince, Hugh C. *Tithe Surveys for Historians.* (Phillimore, 2000).

For a more basic introduction, see:
- Evans, Eric J. *Tithes: Maps, Apportionments and the 1836 Act: A Guide for Local Historians.* (3rd ed., British Association for Local History, 1997).

See also:
- Beech, Geraldine, & Mitchell, Rose. *Maps for Family and Local History: The Records of the Tithe, Valuation Office and National Farm Surveys of England and Wales, 1836–1943.* 2nd ed. (The National Archives, 2004).

Tithe maps and apportionments are fully listed in:
- Kain, Roger J. P., & Oliver, Richard R. *The Tithe Maps of England and Wales: A Cartographic Analysis and County-by-County Catalogue.* (Cambridge University Press, 1995).

Kain has also provided an extensive atlas of land use, based on the tithe files:
- Kain, Roger J.P. *An Atlas and Index of the Tithe Files of Mid-Nineteenth-Century England and Wales.* (Cambridge University Press, 1986).

Welsh researchers will need to consult:
- Davies, Robert. *The Tithe Maps of Wales.* (National Library of Wales, 1999).

A guide to tithe maps online is provided by:
- Tithe and Enclosure Maps
  www.bl.uk/reshelp/findhelprestype/maps/tithemaps/tithemaps.html

A variety of calendars, indexes and databases for particular counties are in print or on the web. These include:

DERBYSHIRE
- Beckett, J.V., & Heath, J.E., eds, *Derbyshire Tithe Files 1836–50.* (Derbyshire Record Society 22, 1995).

ESSEX
- Lockwood, Herbert Hope. *Tithe and Other Records of Essex and Barking: Guide for Family and Local Historians.* (Chelmsford: Essex Record Office, 2006).

HERTFORDSHIRE
- Walker, Jane, ed. *Datchworth Tithe Accounts 1711–1747.* (Hertfordshire Record Publications 25, 2010).
- Doree, Stephen G., ed. *The Parish Register and Tithing Book of Thomas Hassall of Amwell.* (Hertfordshire Record Publications 5, 1989).

NORTHAMPTONSHIRE
- Greenall, R.L. 'The Daventry Tithing Book, 1700–1818', in King, Edmund, ed., *A Northamptonshire Miscellany.* (Northamptonshire Record Society 32, 1983), pp.59–108.

SUSSEX
- Tithe Maps for East Sussex and Brighton & Hove
  www.eastsussex.gov.uk/leisureandtourism/localandfamilyhistory/esro/collections/tithemaps/default.htm

WILTSHIRE
- Sandell, R. E., ed. *Abstracts of Wiltshire Tithe Apportionments.* (Wiltshire Record Society 30, 1975).

WORCESTERSHIRE
- Walker, Peter L., ed. *Tithe Apportionments of Worcestershire, 1837–1851.* (Worcestershire Historical Society, new series 23, 2011 (includes CD)).

Chapter 8

ENCLOSURE AWARDS AND MAPS

Open fields farmed in common were found in many parts of medieval England, but had disappeared by the mid-nineteenth centuries as a result of enclosure. Fencing fields off from each other meant that individual farmers could use their land how they liked, instead of having to conform to collective decisions. Common rights were extinguished: farming ceased to be a communal endeavour and became an individualistic enterprise.

It is possible to trace the progress of enclosure from the mid-sixteenth century by using enclosure awards and their accompanying maps. These documents were generally required by individual Acts of Parliament, which provided legal security for owners of enclosed lands. The majority of Enclosure Acts date from the eighteenth and nineteenth centuries, although the first was passed in 1604. Earlier enclosure was undertaken by agreements enrolled by decree in one of the Westminster courts.

Acts usually authorized commissioners to undertake new enclosures. A few merely confirmed enclosure that had taken place long before. The Higham (Leicestershire) enclosure provides an extreme example. It took place in 1632 and was confirmed by an Act of 1806. Between 1604 and 1914, over 5,000 enclosure bills were enacted, covering about one-fifth of the area of England.

The General Enclosure Act of 1801 simplified the procedure to be followed, reducing the time and expense involved and making maps compulsory. Subsequent Acts usually refer to that Act for model clauses. Further general enclosure Acts followed in 1836, 1840 and 1845, greatly reducing the need for private Acts. The 1845 Act established an Enclosure Commission authorized to make awards without the need for an Act.

Most eighteenth- and nineteenth-century private enclosures began with discussion among landowners and attempts to disarm any potential opposition. This was followed by a public meeting to approve a draft Parliamentary bill and to petition for a private Act. The passage of a bill through Parliament can be followed in the *Commons Journal*, which sometimes gives useful information such as acreages. The procedure followed is outlined by Tate.[1] Local MPs were usually responsible for introducing bills into the House of Commons. A consents form had to be provided to the House, listing all those with any interest in the land concerned and indicating whether they consented, opposed or were neutral to the proposed enclosure. There were also, sometimes, petitions from opponents.

Once an Act had been secured, the commissioners undertook a survey and apportioned the land between all who claimed rights in it. That could take time. The Enclosure Act for Aston (Berkshire) was passed in 1808 but the award was completed in 1817. That was exceptional, but the process sometimes took even longer: at Horton (Gloucestershire) it took eighteen years from the passing of the Act in 1798. Even then, the land had to be fenced and the roads laid out.

The land still had to be farmed whilst enclosure was in progress. Sometimes Acts gave commissioners responsibility for stocking the land and for ploughing and sowing, so that such decisions tied in with the physical labour of planting hedges, digging ditches and laying out new roads.

Awards generally commence with the words 'To all to whom these presents shall come', followed by the names of commissioners and local landowners. They recite the general background, using the words 'And Whereas' to commence each new paragraph. Details of the award follow, commencing with the words 'Now Therefore'. This section is likely to give the old field and other place names. It will also include details of new roads, footpaths, watercourses, quarries and gravel pits. Fencing was fundamental to enclosure, so the award sets out how the new closes were to be fenced, who was to do it and who was to maintain the boundary. Usually the fence was to be quickset (hawthorn) hedge. Ditching was fundamental, since the purpose of the enclosure was to improve the productivity of the land. The position and dimensions of drains will therefore be indicated, together with the names of those responsible for maintenance. Allotments made to finance the costs of enclosure, together with details of any exchanges made between allottees, may be noted. The main body of the award then follows, giving details of new allotments (which are numbered) and the names of those to whom they were allotted.

Everyone who had rights in the lands enclosed, from great landowners to humble cottagers, received an allotment. They are usually listed in order of social rank, beginning with the lord of the manor and proceeding through the rector, the yeomen, the husbandmen and the cottagers. Small allotments were frequently made to the parish overseers in order to keep the poor rate down, and to the church for its maintenance. Land might be set aside for public quarries, for a village pound for stray animals and for other public purposes. The award was completed by being dated, signed and sealed by the commissioners in the presence of an attorney and publicly read before the major parties.

Enclosure maps had no standard format. Some are rolled, some flat and many are quite bulky. Maps were drawn up by surveyors and show how open fields and waste were divided among the landowners. They depict new boundaries, drains and roads. Each close is given its own number, referring back to the number given in the award. Acreages may be given. These do not necessarily correspond to the acreages stated in the Act, since the latter had not been accurately surveyed. There could be dramatic differences: the 1813 Act enclosing Llangynfelyn (Carmarthenshire) stated that there were 10,000 acres; the commissioners only found 4,505. The letter 'T' on the side of a boundary may indicate the owner responsible for its maintenance. Buildings may be depicted, but that was incidental to the purpose of the map: the absence of any indication of a building does not mean that it was not there at the time. The whole parish is not necessarily covered; only that part of it that was being enclosed.

Enclosure maps and awards together show how the open fields were to be enclosed and distributed; the shapes and sizes of the fields; the names of those allotted land; whether consolidated holdings were to be created; how much land was allotted for public use, the glebe, the poor, gravel pits and similar uses; whether properties were exchanged; and how new roads were to be laid out.

Enclosure altered the landscape permanently. Instead of vast expanses of open field, there were numerous hedges and ditches, together with new straight roads and footpaths for access. The effect of enclosure on society has been much debated; certainly it meant the end of popular customs such as gleaning, extinguished common rights to fuel and pasture, made poachers of those who hunted rabbits, and tended to pauperize the poor. Even those who had smallholdings might have to sell up if they could not afford the cost of fencing and ditching the land they were allotted. It was popularly thought that:

> The fault is great in man or woman
> Who steals a goose from off a common,
> But what can plead that man's excuse
> Who steals a common from a goose?

Enclosure had the opposite effect upon the parish clergy. The tithe payable on the lands enclosed was generally commuted in exchange for land.

Securing exemption from tithe was an important, if subsidiary, reason for undertaking enclosure. The land allocated to tithe owners was generally fenced at the expense of other landowners. Between 1757 and 1835, 2,220 Enclosure Acts commuting tithes were passed and over 185,000 acres passed into the ownership of the clergy. The value of the living at Doddington (Cambridgeshire) increased from just over £22 under Henry VIII to no less than £7,000 by the 1840s. Enclosure and drainage of the Fens made a major contribution to the increase, although law suits also helped.[2] Doddington was exceptional but Cowper's 'worthy priest' was no longer to be 'cut like a scythe' at tithing-time. Instead, he could let out his wide acres, achieve the status of a gentleman, and also undermine popular support for the established church.[3]

Vestries and churchwardens rarely had any formal role in enclosure (unless they were trustees of charities holding lands being enclosed). They did, however, serve as custodians of the resultant documents. Most Enclosure Acts provided for the deposit of a map and award in the parish chest, with a copy for the Clerk of the Peace. After 1801, this was always compulsory. Sometimes Enclosure Acts and other relevant papers can be found among parish records. All Acts of Parliament are held by the Parliamentary Archives www.parliament.uk/business/publications/parliamentary-archives, although they sometimes turn up among parish records and elsewhere.

Earlier awards were enrolled in Chancery and other Westminster courts. In Middlesex, Yorkshire and the Isle of Ely they were enrolled in the local deeds registries. Awards enrolled under the 1845 Act can be found not only among parish and county records but also among the records of the Board of Agriculture in The National Archives (class MAF1). Sometimes, local landowners had copies made for their own use and many of these have been deposited with estate archives in local record offices.

Further Reading
The processes of enclosure, together with the records that resulted, are described in much greater detail in:
- Hollowell, S. *Enclosure Records for Historians.* (Phillimore, 2000).
See also:
- Tate, W.E. 'Enclosure Awards and Acts', in Munby, Lionel M., ed. *Short Guides to Records.* (Historical Association, 1972, separately paginated).
Enclosure acts and awards are listed in:
- Tate, W.E. *Domesday of English Enclosure Acts and Awards*, ed. M.E. Turner. (University of Reading Library, 1978).

Enclosure maps are catalogued in:
- Kain, Roger J.P., Chapman, John & Oliver, Richard, *The Enclosure Maps of England and Wales, 1595–1918.* (Cambridge University Press, 2004). This includes an online database at http://hds.essex.ac.uk/em

Enclosure awards and maps at The National Archives are described in:
- Enclosure Awards
  www.nationalarchives.gov.uk/records/research-guides/enclosure.htm

For Wales, see:
- Chapman, John. *Guide to Parliamentary Enclosures in Wales.* (University of Wales Press, 1992).

A guide to enclosure maps online is provided by:
- British Library Help for Researchers: Tithe and Enclosure Maps
  www.bl.uk/reshelp/findhelprestype/maps/tithemaps/tithemaps.html

There are many good accounts of the enclosure movement, only a few of which can be mentioned here. For a basic introduction, see:
- Turner, Michael. *Enclosures in Britain, 1750–1830.* (Macmillan, 1984).

Neeson offers an excellent account for the eighteenth century:
- Neeson, J.M. *Commoners: Common Right, Enclosure and Social Change in England, 1700–1820.* (Cambridge University Press, 1996).

Yelling covers a longer period:
- Yelling, J.A. *Common Field and Enclosure in England 1450–1850.* (Macmillan, 1977).

Two more recent works are:
- Allen, Robert C. *Enclosure and the Yeoman.* (Clarendon Press, 1992).
- Mingay, G.E. *Parliamentary Enclosure in England, 1750–1850: An Introduction to its Causes, Incidence and Impact, 1750–1850.* (Longman, 1997).

The British Library page listed above identifies many online sources. There are also many printed local studies; far too many to list here. However, one excellent example is:
- Russell, Eleanor, & Russell, Rex C. *Landscape Changes in South Humberside: The Enclosures of Thirty-Seven Parishes.* (Humberside Leisure Services, 1982).

Chapter 9

PARISH CHARITIES

The word 'charity' derives from the Latin 'caritas', which can also be translated as 'love'. God's love is at the root of the Christian gospel. One of the primary roles of the church is to act as a channel of that love. All Christians were expected to be charitable; as a minimum they were expected to pay one-tenth of their income in tithe (see Chapter 7). Monks and priests, as recipients of tithe, were expected to distribute a third to the poor.

Very little is known about pre-Reformation charity. No doubt much was given during life, but few records survive. Wills, however, show that most testators made bequests to the poor. Many legacies were undirected largesse; giving to the poor was regarded as giving to God. The cynic might argue that what mattered to testators was that legacies to the poor were thought to reduce the time to be spent in purgatory. Funeral doles were also an important indicator of the social status of the deceased.

The Reformation redirected charitable concerns. Belief in purgatory ceased. Jesus' injunction to give to the poor was reinterpreted, emphasizing the need to avoid misdirection of giving. The government was increasingly concerned about increasing numbers of beggars and the impact they might have on society as a whole. The aims of the church were, as the Webbs put it, 'exactly opposite' to those of the Crown, whose primary concern was the maintenance of order.[1] Nevertheless, the reformers agreed that charity should be directed to where it would do most good; and least harm. It was increasingly expected to be socially responsible. Outcomes became important.

After the Reformation, parishes took on a major role in the official relief of poverty (see Chapter 4). They also became a major conduit for voluntary charitable giving. Collections were frequently taken for the relief of the poor, as well as for briefs (see below). Many benefactors arranged for the charities they founded to be administered by parish officers. By 1660, over 10,000 charitable trusts were in existence. Between 1660 and 1740, the number doubled, perhaps even tripled. The church ale, the funeral dole and the loose change given to the poor in many testators' wills may have withered, but they had been replaced by other charitable gifts.[2]

A Table of Benefactions.
bequeathed to this Parish.

Imprs William Goddard Esq: Built an Hospital.
in the year 1627. wherein he hath provided for
40 poor people for Ever: and left it to the Sole
Care and Government of the Right Worshipful
Company of Fishmongers. of the City of London.
of which Company he was a free Brother: Whereof
there are to be Six Londoners. free of the said
Company. and the Rest of this Parish.

The Most Revd Father in God. William Laud.
Lord Arch Bishop of Canterbury. by his last Will.
charged his Estate. in the said Parish of Bray.
called Stroud. with the payment of ten pounds
yearly for two years in three. for putting out a
poor Boy Apprentice. born in the said Parish.
the Boy to be chosen the 7th day of October.

Doctor Challoner. by his last Will charged his
Estate at East Oakely. in the said Parish of Bray.
with the Payment of Forty Shillings to the poor of
East Oakely. and Bray unto Four of the Godlyest poor:
to be changed yearly. And also he gave out of the
Said Estate. Forty Shillings yearly unto Some
Godly Preacher. to be chosen yearly by his heirs. and
the Dean of Windsor. to preach Six Sermons. on
some Six Sabbaths. in the Parish Church of Bray.
as haveing care on their Souls.

Sr Willm Paul. gave the yearly sum of five pounds
to be Distributed every year. a fortnight before
Christmas. by his Relations who shall be possessed
of his Estate. to such of the poor of the said Parish
of Bray. who are of the Communion of the Church of
England. and his Estate called Kimbers. in
East Oakely. is charged with the payment of the
said Money.

The Benefactors' Board at Bray (Berkshire).

Parish charities performed a variety of roles: educational, poverty relief, health care, etc. They provided doles and food handouts to the poor, free schools, orphanages, apprenticeship premiums and other benefits for the local community. The trustees of the parish lands at Gnosall (Staffordshire) were expected to distribute its revenues in accordance with instructions from the vestry. The money was generally used to pay apprenticeship premiums, legal costs, doctors' bills and deficits on the accounts of overseers and churchwardens.

Charities were frequently founded by bequests. Testators expected some post-mortem control over who was to benefit. They did not intend them to be merged with general parochial funds, even though they were occasionally used to reduce poor rates. Status and social control were prominent aspects of charitable giving. Charity boards recording benefactors' names are common in churches: a board at Bray (Berkshire) records how Dr Challoner left 40s per year to be paid to 'four of the Godlyest poor', plus a further 40s to pay for six sermons from 'Some Godly preacher'. It also records an apprenticeship charity founded by the will of Archbishop Laud.

Poorer testators made small bequests to the church or to the poor, sometimes for distribution by parish officers. Testators at Pittington (Co. Durham) who bequeathed money to the 'stocke of the poor' are memorialized in the churchwardens' accounts, together with the dates of their bequests. The money was used to put the poor to work. Less formal giving was frequently left unrecorded.

Churchwardens became involved in two systems of poor relief: charitable giving based on medieval precedent, and the compulsory system based on the Elizabethan Poor Laws discussed in Chapter 4. Medieval churchwardens' accounts sometimes record church ales that were instigated privately for the support of some charitable purpose.

Records of parish charities were frequently stored in the parish chest. They might include documents such as founders' wills, title deeds, minutes, registers, apprenticeship indentures, etc. The parish records of Uplowman (Devon) include notes on the origins of four different charities, a number of deeds and related memoranda, various charity accounts, and a number of reports on charities published by the Charity Commissioners in the nineteenth century. Some parishes kept separate charity books recording the management of parish benefactions, and showing how their income was distributed. Where parish officers were trustees of an apprenticeship charity, the apprenticeship indentures were usually stored in parish chests. These give the names of the trustees, as well as the names of the apprentice, usually his parents, and the master.[3]

Churchwardens' accounts frequently record details of charity receipts and expenditure. The Ashburton (Devon) accounts record the names of recipients of Hayman's charity: in 1575–6 'the feofees of the londes of Mr Hayman that he gave to the poore for the byeng of shyrtes and smockes dyd geve unto Christopher Stone a shert & Johan Cooke wydowe the smock for our Lady Day quarter'. There were two beneficiaries, always a man and a woman, in each quarter and all their names are recorded.

Memorial of George Taylor's benefaction at Edington (Wiltshire).

Charities did not necessarily fund all of their endeavours. At Great Budworth (Cheshire), the churchwardens administered the parish school as trustees, but their accounts reveal that scholars were expected to pay fees. In 1750, they paid 1s 6d per quarter in order to learn reading and 2s 6d if both reading and writing were required. 'Accompts' could be taught for an additional 4 pence. Those who sought Latin and Greek were charged 5 shillings.

Extracts from the wills of founders are frequently found in account books. The 1804 will of Lydia Hunt of Gandy Street, Exeter, for example, is extracted in an account book from Shobrooke (Devon). She left £100 to the minister and churchwardens, to be invested in the 'Parliamentary funds of the Kingdom'; the interest was to be used to purchase bread for a monthly distribution 'to such poor people of the said parish as shall for the time being be considered the greatest objects of charity'.

In the same account book is an account of the 'stock money' for Shobrooke. This shows that, in 1787, £100 had been placed in the hands of eight different individuals and yielded a few pounds every year. Robert Down was paid a pound every year 'for teaching poor children to read' between 1772 and 1782; 4 guineas was 'distributed among the poor' in 1784.

Charitable concerns are frequently reflected in vestry minutes. The vestry of St Dionis Backchurch in London met on 9 April 1691 to distribute the 'Yearly Guift of ye Lady Harvey'; the names of the recipients were listed.

Where charities held landed property, the deeds were likely to be in the parish chest. A Repton (Derbyshire) inventory of 1630 records: 'xviii Deeds in a boxe, xij of yem sealed and vj without seales.'

Charities were not always run in accordance with their intended purpose. At Stow (Lincolnshire), income from the church lands should have been used to pay for the maintenance of church fabric. Instead, the churchwardens diverted the money to pay routine expenses such as the clerk's wages and wine for Communion. A reforming rector secured a new body of trustees and ensured that the income was used for its proper purpose.[4]

Charities did not always survive. The Charity Commissioners' reports record numerous losses, for a variety of reasons. Money lent out could be lost if the borrower went bankrupt or died without assets. Property could be mismanaged or embezzled by trustees. Overseers and churchwardens sometimes misappropriated funds for which they were responsible in order to reduce the poor rate. At Gnosall (Staffordshire), when the workhouse was built in 1733, it was recorded that:

'tis agreed upon by the Minister Churchwardens and other inhabitants … that ye trustees Belonging to Hencocke's living shall pay ye rents as they receive up into ye hands of ye Churchwardens or overseers … and that ye said rent shall be Imployd to the maintenance of the workhouse.'

The Charity Commission was established in 1853; its remit was to ensure that charities were properly conducted. Commissioners' reports were published in the Parliamentary papers series and most local studies libraries and record offices have copies for their own areas. Sometimes, extracts relating to parochial charities can be found among parish records. They provide much information on local charities.[5]

Medieval giving was encouraged by Papal indulgences. They promised to reduce the time spent in purgatory in return for contributions towards some building project, perhaps a church or a bridge. However, indulgences came under fierce attack from Martin Luther and ceased to be issued in the mid-sixteenth century.

Briefs authorized by popes and bishops played an important role in organized charitable giving before the Reformation. After the Reformation, the state took control of them. None are known for the reigns of Edward VI or Mary, but Queen Elizabeth issued many under her sign manual or privy seal, mostly for the repair of churches. For example, when the church at Shifnal (Shropshire) burnt down in 1592, a brief authorized collections in the counties of Shropshire, Staffordshire, Flintshire and Montgomeryshire.[6] During the Interregnum, briefs were temporarily inhibited by Parliament to prevent the king from raising contributions for his cause. From 1653, many were issued by the Council of State and can be traced among the State Papers Domestic in The National Archives.

The system was reorganized after the Restoration. A brief became a royal warrant, issued under Letters Patent, authorizing collections in church or from house to house; they were printed and could be sent out to every parish in England and Wales. A detailed account of the reasons for the brief was given. Many were issued for the ransom of slaves captured by Barbary pirates, for the relief of the sufferings of Huguenot refugees and for the defence of the 'poor Palatines'. Others recorded major disasters by fire and flood, sometimes giving the names of victims. Briefs did not necessarily attract as much support as a collection for local purposes; nevertheless, they did demonstrate the power of the Crown to mobilize nationwide support for particular causes.[7]

It cost money to obtain a brief. When Wandsworth (Surrey) suffered damage to its church in 1629, it sought a brief to help with the cost of repairs. The cost of obtaining one, recorded in its churchwardens' accounts, was over £3. That included gratuities (or perhaps fees) for the Lord Keeper's porter, for his 'secretaryes man', and for the bishop's porter, as well as surveyors' fees and travel.

The distribution of briefs was a monopoly. Under an Act of Queen Anne, the distributor was to number them before sending them to parish clergy, who read them from the pulpit. After a specified period they were to be returned with contributions received, and the distributor was to prepare his accounts and submit them to the Court of Chancery. For over a century, the distributor was based in Stafford; William Salt was the son of the last distributor and consequently the William Salt Library in Stafford holds a part of the distributor's archive.[8] It includes briefs and warrants, account books, distribution books, lists of parishes, meetings, chapels, instructions and printed forms. The costs involved in the system were heavy and the amounts raised could be minimal. When the Church Building Society began to make grants for the repair of churches in 1818, the need for the system was eroded, and it was abolished in 1828.

A collection of church briefs was presented to the British Museum by another member of the Salt family in 1829.[9] They are accompanied by a handwritten *Inventory of Letters Patent Authorizing the Collection of Alms by Briefs.*

Briefs themselves rarely survive among parish records; they were supposed to be returned to the bishop with a note of the amount collected. However, collections are recorded in churchwardens' accounts and elsewhere. An Act of 1705 required collectors to keep a separate book to record details of briefs received and moneys collected, but this merely required something that was frequently already being done. A 'register of ye Briefes recd and read by me Nath Dalton, Rector, wth ye names of ye Chwardens in whose hands ye Briefes with ye money collected do remain until they are called for' can be found among the Cucklington (Somerset) parish records.

Briefs were read in church, and collections were taken either from those present or by a 'walking collection' in which minister and churchwardens went from door to door. Alternatively, a donation might be made from general church funds. A Bilston (Staffordshire) account book records that in 1688 collections were made for the victims of a fire at Oundle (Northamptonshire) and an earthquake at Kettlewell (Yorkshire). The following year, a house-to-house collection was made for refugee Irish protestants and £2 5s 11d was collected.

Churchwardens' accounts record many briefs. The printed edition of Tavistock (Devon) churchwardens' accounts devotes five pages to listing contributors to 'the redemption of the p'sent captives nowe in Turkey' in 1670.[10] Sometimes briefs authorized collections in places far distant from where the need arose. The churchwardens of High Ercall (Shropshire) collected 6s 3d 'for a fire at South Molton (Devon)' in 1704. That fire also attracted 13 shillings from a Salisbury (Wiltshire) parish.

Briefs did not always attract support, partly because there were too many of them. No fewer than 423 were received at Abbots Ripton (Hertfordshire) between 1709 and 1747. Samuel Pepys commented, as early as 1661, that 'we observe, the trade in briefs is now come up to so constant a course every Sunday, that we are resolved to give no more to them'. Many agreed: for example, at Houghton (Hampshire) in 1795, nine successive briefs produced nothing at all.

The brief authorizing the collection for the rebuilding of St Paul's Cathedral was one of the most successful. Approximately 3,300 parish returns have survived, covering most English and Welsh counties; they are now held at the London Metropolitan Archives.[11] Most list churchwardens and clergy, together with the names of contributors. Although some parishes refused any contribution, other returns can almost serve as lists of the adult inhabitants, especially where they also list those who did not contribute. Some returns indicate the status of the contributors; most record amounts.

Copies of returns were sometimes retained in parish chests, perhaps written into churchwardens' accounts or the parish register. At St Olave's, Hart Street (London), the minister and churchwardens collected from door to door in 1680 and recorded the names of contributors in an account book; the amount raised was over £62.[12]

Church briefs, sometimes known as 'King's briefs' or 'royal briefs', may be confused with 'protections' or 'letters of request' issued by Quarter Sessions. It is not always clear whether a particular collection was made as a result of a brief or a Quarter Sessions order. The latter could be obtained by petitioning Quarter Sessions and proving some great loss or affliction. Quarter Sessions would commend the cause to local clergy and invite them to publish the petition in their churches. In 1768, for example, the Yorkshire West Riding justices agreed 'That the parish church of Farnham is in so ruinous a condition that the inhabitants cannot assemble therein without eminent danger of their lives, and that the same cannot any longer be supported but must be wholly taken down and rebuilt.' They estimated the cost at over £1,135 'which the said inhabitants are unable to raise among themselves, being chiefly tenants at rack rents and burthened with a numerous poor'. House-to-house collections throughout Yorkshire and Lancashire were authorized for this purpose.

More local suffering might be relieved by the parish or neighbouring parishes without outside intervention. In the seventeenth century, George Herbert argued that if 'God have sent any calamity either by fire or famine to any neighbouring Parish', the country parson

'expects no Briefe; but taking his Parish together the next Sunday ... and exposing to them the uncertainty of humane affairs, none knowing whose turne may be next, and then when he hath affrighted them with this exposing the obligation of Charity and Neighbour-hood, he first gives himself liberally and then incites them to give.'[13]

In similar vein, when a 1714 fire in a Bilston (Staffordshire) 'hatchelling shop' caused damage estimated at £80, the chapel wardens collected £3 4s 9½d to assist the victim.

Further Reading

Charity is one aspect of gift-giving and reciprocity. Its history is placed in context by:

- Ben-Amos, Ilana Krausman. *The Culture of Giving: Informal Support and Gift-Exchange in Early Modern England.* (Cambridge University Press, 2008).

For a heavily-criticized but nevertheless invaluable overview of the history of charity in England, see:

- Jordan, W.K. *Philanthropy in England 1480–1660: A Study of the Changing Pattern of English Social Aspirations.* (George Allen & Unwin, 1959). This is one of a series of books examining the history of giving in the regions.

A more recent history of charities in London is provided by:

- Schen, Claire S. *Charity and Lay Piety in Reformation London, 1500–1620.* (Ashgate, 2002).

Legal aspects of local charities are discussed in:

- Alvey, Martin. *From Chantry to Oxfam: A Short History of Charity and Charity Legislation.* (British Association for Local History, 1995).

For an introduction to the use of briefs, which includes an extensive list of publications mentioning them, see:

- Harris, Mark. 'The Finding and Use of Brief Records', *Archives* 21, 1994, pp.129–44.

See also:

- Harris, Mark. 'Inky Blots and Rotten Parchment Bonds: London, Charity Briefs, and the Guildhall Library', *Historical Research* 66, 1993, pp.98–110.

For more detailed introduction to briefs, see:

- Bewes, W.A. *Church Briefs or Royal Warrants for Collections for Charitable Objects.* 1896.

For a useful introduction, together with the accounts of briefs from a Staffordshire parish, see:

- Laithwaite, P. *The Parish Briefs of Bilston* (Collections for a History of Staffordshire, 3rd series, 1938), pp.203–63 & 336–44.

For transcripts from a collection of Yorkshire briefs, see:

- 'Yorkshire Briefs', *Yorkshire Archaeological Journal* 16, 1902, pp.114–20; 17, 1903, pp.59–71.

Chapter 10

OTHER MISCELLANEOUS RECORDS

A wide variety of other records was sometimes stored in parish chests; for example, local census returns, deeds and other records of property owned by the church, Acts of Parliament, proclamations, extracts from the *London Gazette*, legal papers and other official documents. Stray papers relating to taxes such as the hearth tax and the poll tax were sometimes deposited. Some of the more commonly-held documents are discussed here, but a comprehensive listing would be impossible.

Title Deeds

Many parishes, especially in urban areas, had endowments of lands and quit rents. The title deeds of such property (including endowments of parish charities) can frequently be found among parish records. Much was lost, especially during the Reformation, when property used to fund 'superstitious purposes' was seized by the crown. Much, however, remained; during the reign of Elizabeth, All Saints, Bristol was able to recover much of the property it had lost. Its collection of fifteenth- and early-sixteenth-century deeds is exceptionally extensive.[1] These documents provide clear evidence that the churchwardens understood the wisdom of retaining in their possession proof of title to the parish's rents and properties.

Property could be acquired by bequests, donations and sometimes by purchase. After the dissolution, Romsey (Hampshire) purchased the abbey church for its own use, paying £100; the sale deed, dated 1544, is among its parish records. St Olave's, Hart Street (London) possesses no really ancient deeds. There is, however, a register of deeds relating to the parish estates. Many relate to parish charities. If a church possessed substantial property, then it was sensible to maintain such registers.

There are a wide variety of different types of deeds: for example, feoffments, letters patent, quitclaims, bargains and sale, leases and releases, final concords. All of these may occur among parish records. For a useful brief guide, see:

- Wormleighton, Tim. *Title Deeds for Family Historians.* (Family History Partnership, 2012).

More detail is provided in:

- Alcock, N.W. *Old Title Deeds: A Guide for Local and Family Historians.* 2nd ed. (Phillimore, 2001).

Presentments

One of the duties of both churchwardens and constables was to make presentments at visitations and at Quarter Sessions. These can generally be found among diocesan and Quarter Sessions records and, strictly speaking, are outside the scope of this book. Occasionally, however, copies of presentments and papers relating to them can be found among parish records.

Churchwardens made their presentments at visitations of their archdeacon or bishop. They reported on matters related to church fabric and furnishings, ministry, the morals of parishioners and the orthodoxy of clergy. Recusancy, drunkenness, defamation, misbehaviour in church and sexual offences could all be subjects of churchwardens' presentments. Such presentments were the prime means by which the diocesan hierarchy kept in touch with what was happening in the parishes; bishops and archdeacons had no other means of undertaking investigations. They issued books of articles showing what matters should be presented.[2] As was seen in Chapter 2, however, churchwardens did not necessarily present everything they should have done.[3] Churchwardens' loyalties were primarily to their neighbours, who were frequently not presented when they should have been. In the House of Commons in 1571, they were accused of being more prepared 'to incurre the danger of perjurie than displease some of their neighbours'.

Constables made presentments both to Quarter Sessions and Assizes. Drunkenness, swearing, theft, recusancy and other crimes all came within their purview. So did neglected highways and bridges in need of repair. Householders who neglected to repair pavements in front of their houses, drivers who caused obstruction with carts and wagons or those who caused any kind of 'nuisance', all were regularly presented by the Coventry constables, who also looked out for fire hazards such as thatched roofs, dangerous chimneys and wooden kilns. They checked up on alehouses and brewers, and on tradesmen who had not served an apprenticeship and were therefore not entitled to trade.

A number of collections of presentments have been published. These include:

- Leatherbarrow, J.S. *Churchwardens' Presentments in the Diocese of Worcester c.1660–1760.* (Worcestershire Historical Society occasional publication 1, 1977).
- Johnstone, Hilda, ed. *Churchwardens' Presentments (17th Century).* 2 vols. (Sussex Record Society 50, 1947–9. Pt. 1, Archdeaconry of Chichester. Pt. 2, Archdeaconry of Lewes).
- Peyton, Sidney A., ed. *The Churchwardens' Presentments in the Oxfordshire Peculiars of Dorchester, Thame and Banbury.* (Oxfordshire Record Society 10, 1928).
- Fox, Levi, ed. *Coventry Constables' Presentments 1629–1742* (Dugdale Society 34, 1986).

Local Census Listings

Listings of inhabitants are frequently found among parish records. Some, such as rate lists, Easter books, pew lists and tithe awards, have already been discussed. Others were compiled for a variety of purposes. Many derived from the official census. The enumerators of 1801, 1811, 1821 and 1831 frequently compiled lists of names, depositing them in parish chests before making their returns, despite the fact that these were not required officially.

Proposals for the official census were made many years before the first one was conducted. It is therefore not surprising that unofficial attempts were sometimes made to compile parish enumerations. A few of these survive, such as the 1599 'census' of Ealing. More common are the visiting books compiled by incumbents, used as aides-mémoire as they went around their parishes. Other listings were made for a variety of reasons.

Not all of these listings were preserved in parish chests; some are to be found among Quarter Sessions records and among private estate records. Detailed listings are provided by:
- Chapman, Colin R. *Pre-1841 Censuses & Population Listings in the British Isles.* 5th ed. (Lochin Publishing, 1998).
- Gibson, Jeremy & Medlycott, Mervyn. *Local Census Listings 1522–1930: Holdings in the British Isles.* 3rd ed. (Federation of Family History Societies, 1997).

Schedules deriving from the official census 1801–31 are listed in:
- Wall, Richard, Woollard, Matthew & Moring, Beatrice. *Census Schedules and Listings 1801–1831: An Introduction and Guide.* (University of Essex Department of History, 2004). Updated at www.essex.ac.uk/history/Staff_Research/working-papers/MW-RW-BM.pdf

A number of incumbents' visiting books are printed in:
- Hurley, Beryl, ed. *Incumbents' Visiting Books.* (Wiltshire Family History Society, 1994).

Notices and Proclamations

Sunday services before the age of mass communication were also public meetings and were used as such. When the Crown wished to communicate with its subjects, it did so via the parish church. Parish chests sometimes contained numerous proclamations and other public notices. These covered a wide diversity of subjects: fasts, thanksgivings, public morals, blasphemy and defence. Among the Steeple Ashton (Wiltshire) parish records there are seventeen proclamations and printed forms relating to preparations against Napoleon's threatened invasion of 1799–1801. The Meshaw (Devon) parish records include a 1742 proclamation of a general fast. Public thanksgivings were frequently proclaimed: the peace concluded with the French king in 1713 and a 'signal and glorious victory in Spain' in 1710 were both the subjects of thanksgiving proclamations among the parish records of St Peter's, Ipswich (Suffolk). Such proclamations were frequently accompanied by special forms of prayer (see Chapter 5).

More local matters also had to be announced in church. After 1744, enclosure bills had to be published in the parish church before consideration in Parliament. Other public notices were increasingly given in church. Sometimes they were also pinned to the church door. The Parish Notices Act of 1837 ended the practice of making such announcements and forbade ministers from giving any notices other than banns of marriage and notices required by crown or bishop. Other notices were to be attached to the church door.

Acts of Parliament

Copies of Acts of Parliament are frequently to be found among parish records. Local Acts were commonly held, especially Enclosure Acts. Clergy and parish officers needed to consult Acts which bore on their responsibilities; those relating to the keeping of parish registers were frequently acquired. Coln Rogers (Gloucestershire) has the 1678 Act for Burying in Woollen. Meshaw (Devon) has Lord Hardwicke's Marriage Act of 1753. Other topics were also covered: Heavitree (Devon) has printed abstracts of the Highway Acts dated 1833 and a copy of the Vestry Act 1818; Brampford Speke (Devon) has a copy of the Parish Notices Act 1837.

The King's Evil

The commonly-accepted treatment for scrofula prior to the reign of George I was to be touched by the monarch; hence its popular name, the King's Evil. It has been calculated that 90,978 people were touched by Charles II between 1660 and 1683.[4] Touching was carried out ritualistically, in accordance with a ceremony that remained unchanged for almost two centuries after 1509. Sufferers had to obtain a certificate from their parish priest and churchwardens before they could be admitted to the king's presence. Ministers were required to keep a list of the certificates they had issued and these sometimes survive among parish records. The parish register of Petworth (Sussex) lists certificates issued in the 1680s. Sometimes churchwardens paid a sufferer's travelling costs. At Seal (Surrey), a rate raised 9 shillings to assist sufferers to visit the royal court: 'To Will'm Giles for his charitie and travel to London with Widowe Hilles children to be cured of the King's evill, by a rate for that cause made by the parishe as appears under divers of their hands.' The cost of travel from Devon was much higher: it cost Tavistock £2 6s 3d to send Eliseus Cruse to London 'to bee touched' in 1662.

Further Reading
• Bloch, Marc. *The Royal Touch: Sacred Monarchy and Scrofula in England and France.* (Routledge & Kegan Paul, 1973).

Other Records
This book has far from exhausted the range of sources that used to be held in parish chests. Hawkhurst (Kent), for example, possesses a book entitled 'Copies of Divers Patents, Graunts and other deeds etc touching Wye, Hawkhurst etc'. Among the documents copied are a decree from Archbishop Warham regarding who paid for the surplice, an acquittance for £125 received from Mr George Courthope, a grant of the rectory of Hawkhurst to the Duke of Suffolk, the will of Thomas Eddenden and a wide range of other deeds. Similarly, at Lacock (Wiltshire) a collection of Quarter Sessions orders enables the history of the parish's bridges to be reconstructed.

In earlier centuries, the parish chest frequently served as a safe deposit for parishioners and was used to store valuable personal papers such as deeds and apprenticeship indentures. More recently, many parishes have records of Sunday schools, youth clubs and other church organizations. Much remains to be explored; twentieth-century parish records in particular have rarely been seen by researchers.

NOTES

Chapter 1: What Can You Do With Parish Records?

1. Morris, Richard. *Churches in the Landscape.* (J.M. Dent & Sons, 1989), p.374.
2. Bruce, John. 'Extracts from Accounts of the Churchwardens of Minchinhampton in the County of Gloucester with Observations Thereon', *Archaeologia* 35, 1853, pp.414–8.
3. Durrant, Peter, ed. *Berkshire Overseers' Papers, 1654–1834.* (Berkshire Record Society 3, 1997), pp.xiii–xiv.
4. See, for example, Hitchcock, Tim, King, Peter & Sharpe, Pamela, eds. *Chronicling Poverty: The Voices and Strategies of the English Poor, 1640–1840.* (Palgrave, 1997).
5. Burgess, Clive, ed. *The Church Records of St Andrew Hubbard Eastcheap c.1350–c1570.* (London Record Society 34, 1999), p.xxix.
6. Burgess, Clive, ed. *The Pre-Reformation Records of All Saints' Church, Bristol*, Part I. (Bristol Record Society 46, 1995), pp.xviii, xxxi & passim.

Chapter 2: The English Parish and its Government

1. Kümin, Beat A. *The Shaping of a Community: The Rise and Reformation of the English Parish, c.1400–1560.* (Scolar Press, 1996), p.178.
2. *Taxatio ecclesiastica Angliae et Walliae auctoritate P.Nicholae IV circa 1291.* Record Commissioners, 1802.
3. Church Statistics 2010/11 www.churchofengland.org/media/1477827/2010_11churchstatistics.pdf
4. Kümin, *Shaping of a Community*, op. cit., pp.193 & 195.
5. Jones, Anthea. *A Thousand Years of the English Parish: Medieval Patterns and Modern Interpretations.* (Windrush Press, 2000), p.154.
6. Evans, Eric J. *The Contentious Tithe: The Tithe Problem and English Agriculture, 1750–1850.* (Routledge & Kegan Paul, 1976), pp.8–9.
7. Watts, Sylvia, ed. *Staffordshire Glebe Terriers, 1585–1884*, Pt.1. Collections for a History of Staffordshire, 4th series, 22. (Staffordshire Record Society, 2009), p.23.
8. For Cornish references in the following paragraphs, see Potts, Richard, ed. *A Calendar of Cornish Glebe Terriers 1673–1735.* (Devon & Cornwall Record Society, new series 19, 1974).
9. Macfarlane, Alan, ed. *The Diary of Ralph Josselin 1616–1683.* (Oxford University Press, 1976).

10. Barratt, D.M., ed. *Ecclesiastical Terriers of Warwickshire Parishes.* (Dugdale Society 22, 1956), p.xxxiii.

11. Quoted by Evans, *Contentious Tithe*, op. cit., p.79.

12. Ibid., pp.105–06.

13. Best, G.F.A. *Temporal Pillars: Queen Anne's Bounty, the Ecclesiastical Commissioners, and the Church of England.* (Cambridge University Press, 1964).

14. Watts, ed. *Staffordshire Glebe Terriers*, op. cit., p.5.

15. Evans, *Contentious Tithe*, op. cit., p.3.

16. Ransome, Mary, ed. *Wiltshire Returns to the Bishop's Visitation Queries, 1783.* (Wiltshire Record Society 27, 1972), pp.9–11.

17. Kümin, *Shaping of a Community*, op. cit., p.133.

18. See especially Venn, J. & Venn, J.A. *Alumni Cantabrigiensis*, Pt. 1 (4 vols) 1250–1751. Pt. 2 (6 vols) 1751–1900 (Cambridge University Press, 1922–54), and Foster, Joseph. *Alumni Oxonienses: The Members of the University of Oxford, 1500–1714 … 4* vols (James Parker, 1891). A further 4 vols cover the period 1715–1886. A variety of other biographical dictionaries of university students are listed in Raymond, Stuart A. *Occupational sources for genealogists.* 2nd ed. (Federation of Family History Societies, 1996). Some of these are now available online.

19. For canon law, see Bray, Gerald, ed. *The Anglican Canons, 1529–1947.* (Church of England Record Society 6, 1998).

20. Kümin, *Shaping of a Community*, op.cit., p.48.

21. Tate, W.E. *The Parish Chest.* 3rd ed. reprinted. (Phillimore, 1983), p.14.

22. For the London information in the following paragraphs, see Merritt, J.F. 'Contested Legitimacy and the Ambiguous Rise of Vestries in Early Modern London', *Historical Journal* 54(1), 2011.

23. Ibid., p.28.

24. On the selection of parish officers, see Langelüddecke, Henrik.'"The pooreste and sympleste sorte of people"? The selection of parish officers during the personal rule of Charles I', *Historical Research* 80(208), 2007, pp.225–60.

25. Quoted by Carlson, Eric.'The Origins, Function, and Status of Churchwardens, with Particular Reference to the Diocese of Ely', in Spufford, Margaret, ed. *The World of Rural Dissenters, 1520–1725.* (Cambridge University Press, 1995), p.190.

26. For a study of women churchwardens, see French, Katherine,'Women Churchwardens in Late Medieval England', in Burgess, Clive & Duffy, Eamon, eds. *The Parish in Late Medieval England: Proceedings of the 2002 Harlaxton Symposium.* (Shaun Tyas, 2006), pp.302–21.

27. Kümin, *Shaping of a Community,* pp.31–2.
28. Carlson, 'Origins', pp.185 & 187.
29. Williams, John Foster, ed. *The Early Churchwardens' Accounts of Hampshire.* (Winchester, Warren & Son, 1913), p.xii.
30. For the origins of churchwardens, see Drew, Charles. *Early Parochial Organization in England: The Origins of the Office of Churchwarden.* (St Anthony's Press, 1954).
31. Carlson, 'Origins', op. cit., p.169.
32. Drew, *Early Parochial Organization,* op. cit., p.7.
33. Alldridge, Nick, 'Loyalty and Identity in Chester Parishes, 1540–1640' in Wright, ed. *Parish, Church and People: Local Studies in Lay Religion.* (Hutchinson, 1988), p.107.
34. Herbert, George. *A Priest to the Temple, or, The Country Parson, His Character and Rule of Holy Life.* (T. Garthwait, 1652), Chapter 29.
35. Listed by Burn, Richard. *The Justice of the Peace and Parish Officer.* 7th ed. (E. Richardson & C. Lintoy, 1762), pp.279–80.
36. Ibid., p.278.
37. Bullett, Maggie. 'The Reception of the Elizabethan Religious Settlement in Three Yorkshire Parishes', *Northern History* 48, 2011, pp.241–4.
38. Steel, Thomas, ed. *Prescot Churchwardens Accounts 1635–1663.* (Record Society for Lancashire and Cheshire, 137, 2002), p.xxi.
39. Webb, Sidney & Webb, Beatrice. *English Local Government From the Revolution to the Municipal Corporations Act: The Parish and the County.* (Longmans Green & Co., 1906), p.166.
40. Snell, K.D.M. *Parish and Belonging: Community, Identity and Welfare in England and Wales, 1700–1950.* (Cambridge University Press, 2006), p.349.
41. Philips, David & Storch, Robert D. *Policing Provincial England, 1829–1856: The Politics of Reform.* (Leicester University Press, 1999), p.14.
42. Quoted by Wrightson, Keith, 'Two Concepts of Order: Justices, Constables and Jurymen in Seventeenth-Century England', in Brewer, John & Styles, John, eds. *An Ungovernable People: The English and Their Law in the Seventeenth and Eighteenth Centuries.* (Hutchinson, 1980), p.21.
43. Kent, Joan R. *The English Village Constable 1580–1642: A Social and Administrative Study.* (Clarendon Press, 1986), p.27.
44. Philips, Storch. *Policing Provincial England,* op. cit, pp.17–18 & 56–7.
45. Potts, op.cit., pp.xxvi & 117.
46. Watts, ed. *Staffordshire Glebe Terriers,* op. cit., pp.23–4.
47. Transcribed in Burgess, Clive, ed. *The Pre-Reformation Records of All Saints' Church, Bristol.* Part I. (Bristol Record Society 46, 1995).

48. Brown, Mike. *Guide to Churchwardens' Accounts: A Practical Guide for Family Historians.* (Dartmoor Press, 1997), p.85.

Chapter 3: Vestry Minutes and Officers' Accounts

1. Many citations to original documents in this chapter are taken from the published editions listed on pp.86-7. See also Cox, J. Charles. *Churchwardens' Accounts from the Fourteenth Century to the Close of the Seventeenth Century* (Methuen & Co., 1913).
2. Quoted by French, Katherine L. *The People of the Parish: Community Life in a Late Medieval English Diocese.* (University of Pennsylvania Press, 2001), p.46.
3. Longley, Katherine M. 'The Scottish Incursions of 1327: A Glimpse of the Aftermath (Wigton Church Accounts 1328–9)', *Transactions of the Cumberland & Westmorland Antiquarian & Archaeological Society* 83, 1983, pp.63–72. See also Godwin, Jeremy, 'The Wigton Church Accounts 1328–9: A Translation into English', *Transactions of the Cumberland & Westmorland Antiquarian & Archaeological Society* 3rd series, 7, 2007, pp.85–94.
4. Burn, Richard. *The Justice of the Peace and Parish Officer.* 7th ed. (E. Richardson & C. Lintoy, 1762), p.20.
5. For this and subsequent references to St Ewen's, see Masters, Betty R. & Ralph, Elizabeth, eds. *The Church Book of St Ewen's Bristol, 1454–1584.* (Bristol & Gloucestershire Archaeological Society Records Section 6, 1969).
6. Brushfield, T.N. 'The Churchwardens' Accounts of East Budleigh', *Devonshire Association … Transactions* 26, 1894, p.344; Brown, Mike, *Guide to Churchwardens' Accounts: A Practical Guide for Family Historians.* (Dartmoor Press, 1997), pp.38 & 116. Many references to Devon accounts below are given by Brown.
7. For this and subsequent references to St Andrew Hubbard, see Burgess, Clive, ed. *The Church Records of St Andrew Hubbard Eastcheap c.1350–c.1570.* (London Record Society 34, 1999).
8. Whiting, Robert. *The Blind Devotion of the People: Popular Religion and the English Reformation.* (Cambridge University Press, 1989), p.55.
9. Kümin, Beat A. *The Shaping of a Community: The Rise and Reformation of the English Parish, c.1400–1560.* (Scolar Press, 1996), p.155.
10. French, *People of the Parish*, op. cit., p.103.
11. Raymond, Stuart A. *The Wills of our Ancestors.* (Pen & Sword, 2012), pp.3–4 & 36.
12. Translated by Hardy, W.J. 'Remarks on the History of Seat Reservation in Churches', *Archaeologia* 53, 1890, p.96.
13. For this and subsequent references to Boxford, see Northeast, Peter,

ed. *Boxford Churchwardens' Accounts 1530–1561.* (Suffolk Records Society 23, 1982).

14. French, *People of the Parish*, op. cit., p.127.
15. Johnston, Alexandra F. & MacLean, Sally-Beth. 'Reformation and Resistance in Thames/Severn Parishes: The Dramatic Witness' in French, Katherine L., Gibbs, Gary G. & Kümin, Beat A., eds. *The Parish in English Life, 1400–1600.* (Manchester University Press, 1997), p.188.
16. Cited by Bettey, J.H. *Church and Parish: A Guide for Local Historians.* (Batsford, 1987), p.100.
17. Farnhill, Ken. 'Religious Policy and Parish "Conformity": Cratfield's Lands in the Sixteenth Century' in French, Katherine L., Gibbs, Gary G. & Kümin, Beat A. eds, *The Parish in English Life, 1400–1600.* (Manchester University Press, 1997), p.226.
18. Duffy, Eamon. *Saints, Sacrilege and Sedition: Religion and Conflict in the Tudor Reformations.* (Bloomsbury, 2012), p.112.
19. Alldridge, Nick. 'Loyalty and Identity in Chester Parishes, 1540–1640' in Wright, S.J., ed. *Parish, Church and People: Local Studies in Lay Religion, 1350–1750.* (Hutchinson, 1988), p.92.
20. For the following paragraphs, see Bennett, John Charles. *The English Anglican Practice of Pew Renting, 1800–1960.* University of Birmingham PhD thesis, 2011, p.119, see http://etheses.bham.ac.uk/2864
21. These are discussed in Salzman, L.F. *Building in England Down to 1540: A Documentary History*, Oxford Reprints ed. (Clarendon Press, 1967).
22. Duffy, Eamon. *The Stripping of the Altars, 1400–1580.* 2nd ed. (Yale University Press, 2005), p.484.
23. Bullett, Maggie. 'The reception of the Elizabethan religious settlement in three Yorkshire parishes', *Northern History* 48, 2011, p.238.
24. Queen Elizabeth's orders of 1560–61; cf. Cox, *Churchwardens' Accounts*, op. cit., p.236.
25. Quoted by Duffy, *Saints, Sacrilege and Sedition*, op. cit., p.18.
26. Brushfield, T.N. 'On the Destruction of Vermin in Rural Parishes', *Devonshire Association … Transactions*, 29, 1897, pp.307–08.
27. Gibbs, Gary. 'New Duties for the Parish Community in Tudor London' in French, Katherine L., Gibbs, Gary G. & Kümin, Beat A., eds, *The Parish in English Life, 1400–1600.* (Manchester University Press, 1997), p.171.
28. Webb, Sidney & Webb, Beatrice. *The Story of the King's Highway.* English Local Government 5 (Frank Cass & Co., 1963), pp.51–61.
29. www.leicestershirevillages.com/seagrave/highwaysurveyorsaccounts.html
30. These are listed in Gibson, Jeremy & Dell, Alan. *The Protestation Returns 1641–42 and Other Contemporary Listings.* (Federation of Family History Societies, 2004).

31. On these, see Smith, Toulmin. *English Gilds: The Original Ordinances of 100 English Gilds.* Early English Text Society 40, 1870; Westlake, H.F., *The Parish Gilds of Medieval England.* (SPCK Publishing, 1919).

32. Swayne, Henry James Fowle, ed. *Churchwardens' Accounts of S. Edmund & S. Thomas, Sarum, 1443– 1702, With Other Documents.* (Wiltshire Record Society, 1896), pp.248–72.

33. Basing, Patricia, ed. *Parish Fraternity Register: Fraternity of the Holy Trinity and Ss Fabian and Sebastian (Parish of St Botolph without Aldersgate).* (London Record Society 18, 1982), see www.british-history.ac.uk/source.aspx?pubid=591

Chapter 4: The Poor Law

1. This chapter depends heavily on the works listed at its end, most of which are not further cited here.

2. Slack, Paul. *Poverty and Policy in Tudor and Stuart England.* (Longman, 1988), p.13.

3. Darlington, Ida. ed. *London Consistory Court Wills, 1492–1547.* (London Record Society 3, 1967), p.7.

4. Slack, *Poverty and Policy*, op. cit., p.44.

5. Webb, Sidney & Webb, Beatrice. *English Local Government: English Poor Law History, Part 1: The Old Poor Law.* (Longmans Green & Co., 1927), p.48.

6. Hindle, Steve. *On the Parish?: The Micro-Politics of Poor Relief in Rural England c.1550–1750.* (Clarendon Press, 2004), p.83.

7. Snell, K.D.M. *Parish and Belonging: Community, Identity and Welfare in England and Wales, 1700–1950.* (Cambridge University Press, 2006), p.17.

8. Hindle, *On the Parish?*, op. cit., p.50.

9. Cited ibid., p.384.

10. Slack, *Poverty and Policy*, op. cit., p.84.

11. From 1697 only those paying rates on property valued at over £10 had settlement.

12. Lees, Lynn Hollen. *The Solidarities of Strangers: The English Poor Laws and the People, 1700–1948.* (Cambridge University Press, 1998), pp.79–81.

13. Eccles, Audrey. 'Pretending to be Seafaring Men: Vagrancy Laws and Forgery with Special Reference to Eighteenth-Century Dorset', *Proceedings of the Dorset Natural History and Archaeological Society* 133, 2012, p.4.

14. Slack, *Poverty and Policy*, op. cit., p.97.

15. Ibid., p.94.

16. A wool carder, employed in the cloth trade.

17. Hembry, Phyllis, ed. *Calendar of Bradford on Avon Settlement Examinations and Removal Orders 1725–98.* (Wiltshire Record Society 46, 1990), p.58. This is a summary of the original.
18. Lees, *The Solidarities of Strangers,* op. cit., p.51.
19. Webb, *English Poor Law History,* op. cit., p.309.
20. Ibid., p.xxii.
21. These are discussed in King, Peter, 'Pauper Inventories and the Material Lives of the Poor in the Eighteenth and Early Nineteenth Centuries', in Hitchcock, Tim, King, Peter & Sharpe, Pamela, eds. *Chronicling Poverty: The Voices and Strategies of the English Poor 1640–1840* (Macmillan, 1997), pp.155–91.
22. Webb, *English Poor Law History,* op. cit., p.121.
23. Carter, Paul, ed. *Bradford Poor Law Union: Papers and Correspondence with the Poor Law Commission, October 1834–January 1839.* (Yorkshire Archaeological Society record series 157, 2004), p.xv.
24. Michael Dalton, quoted by Hindle, *On the Parish?,* op. cit., p.218.
25. Ibid., p.207.
26. Webb, *English Poor Law History,* op. cit., p.165.
27. Broad, John. 'Housing the Rural Poor in Southern England 1650–1850', *Agricultural History Review* 48(2), 2000, pp.161–2.
28. Hindle, *On the Parish?,* op. cit., p.64.
29. Slack, *Poverty and Policy,* op. cit., p.92.
30. See Chapter 6 of Snell, K.D.M. *Parish and Belonging: Community, Identity and Welfare in England and Wales, 1700–1950.* (Cambridge University Press, 2006) for overseers' responsibilities after 1834.
31. Ben-Amos, Ilana Krausman. *The Culture of Giving: Informal Support and Gift-Exchange in Early Modern England.* (Cambridge University Press, 2008), p.86.
32. Cited by Hindle, *On the Parish?* op. cit., p.143.
33. Ben-Amos, *Culture of Giving,* op. cit., p.83.

Chapter Five: Records Relating to the Church

1. Listed in *Exchequer (K.R.) Church Goods,* List & Index Society, 69 & 76. 1971–2.
2. Citations are taken from the works listed on pp. 116-7.
3. Ford, Judy Ann. 'Marginality and the Assimilation of Foreigners in the Lay Parish Community: The Case of Sandwich', in French, Katherine L., Gibbs, Gary G., & Kümin, Beat A., eds. *The Parish in English Life, 1400–1600.* (Manchester University Press, 1997), p.212.
4. Potts, Richard, ed. *A Calendar of Cornish Glebe Terriers, 1673–1735.* (Devon & Cornwall Record Society, new series 19, 1974), p.ix.

5. Ibid., p.ix.
6. For the following paragraphs, see the published editions of terriers listed on p.120.
7. On this, see Wright, Catherine. *The Spatial Ordering of Community in English Church Seating, 1550–1700*. University of Warwick PhD thesis, 2002.
http://wrap.warwick.ac.uk/3079/1/WRAP_THESIS_Wright_2002.pdf
8. Cited by Pounds, N.J.G. *A History of the English Parish: The Culture of Religion from Augustine to Victoria.* (Cambridge University Press, 2000), p.477.
9. Ibid., p.477.
10. Cited by ibid., p.477.
11. There are several modern editions; for example, Gough, Richard. *The History of Myddle*, with introduction by Peter Razzell. (Caliban Books, 1979).
12. For the texts of such prayers, see Clay, William Keatinge, ed. *Liturgies and Occasional Forms of Prayer set forth in the Reign of Queen Elizabeth.* (Parker Society 29, 1847).

Chapter Six: Parish Registers of Baptisms, Marriages and Burials
1. Burn, Richard. *The Justice of the Peace and Parish Officer*. 7th ed. (E. Richardson & C. Lintoy, 1762), p.278.
2. Ibid., p.278.

Chapter Seven: Tithe Records
1. Cited by Pounds, N.J.G. *A History of the English Parish: The Culture of Religion from Augustine to Victoria.* (Cambridge University Press, 2000), p.46.
2. Kain, Roger J.P. & Oliver, Richard R. *The Tithe Maps of England and Wales: A Cartographic Analysis and County-by-County Catalogue.* (Cambridge University Press, 1995), p.1.
3. Povah, Alfred. *Annals of the Parishes of St Olave, Hart Street and All Hallows, Staining, in the City of London.* (Blades, East & Blades, 1894), p.244.
4. Pounds, *History of the English Parish*, op. cit., pp.146–7.
5. Evans, Eric J. *The Contentious Tithe: The Tithe Problem and English Agriculture, 1750–1850.* (Routledge & Kegan Paul, 1976), p.95.
6. McClatchey, Diana. *Oxfordshire Clergy 1777–1869: A Study of the Established Church and of the Role of its Clergy in Local Society.* (Clarendon Press, 1960), p.98.
7. Hobbs, Steven, ed. *Wiltshire Glebe Terriers.* (Wiltshire Record Society 56, 2003), p.xiv.

8. Evans, *Contentious Tithe*, op. cit., p.45.
9. Cited by Barratt, D.M., ed. *Ecclesiastical Terriers of Warwickshire Parishes.* (Dugdale Society 22, 1956), p.xix.
10. Evans, Nesta. 'Tithe Books as a Source for the Local Historian', *Local Historian* 14, 1980, p.26.
11. Cited by Evans, *Contentious Tithe*, op. cit., p.67.
12. Ibid., p.155.

Chapter Eight: Enclosure Awards and Maps

1. Tate, W.E. *Domesday of English Enclosure Acts and Awards*, ed. M.E. Turner. (University of Reading Library, 1978), pp.23–8.
2. Best, G.F.A. *Temporal Pillars: Queen Anne's Bounty, the Ecclesiastical Commissioners, and the Church of England.* (Cambridge University Press, 1964), pp.64–5.
3. Jones, Anthea. *A Thousand Years of the English Parish: Medieval Patterns & Modern Interpretations.* (Windrush Press, 2000), p.159.

Chapter Nine: Parish Charities

1. Webb, Sidney, & Webb, Beatrice. *English Poor Law History, Part 1: The Old Poor Law.* (Frank Cass & Co., 1963), p.23.
2. Ben-Amos, Ilana Krausman. *The Culture of Giving: Informal Support and Gift-Exchange in Early Modern England.* (Cambridge University Press, 2008), pp.118 & 379.
3. See Raymond, Stuart A. *My Ancestor was an Apprentice: How Can I Find Out More About Him?* (Society of Genealogists, 2010) for a detailed discussion.
4. Spurrell, Mark, ed. *Stow Church Restored 1846–1866.* (Lincoln Record Society 75, 1984), pp.xx–xxi.
5. It is also worth consulting the parish volumes of the *Victoria County History* for information on parish charities.
6. Laithwaite, P. 'The Parish Briefs of Bilston', *Collections for a History of Staffordshire* 1938, p.206.
7. Ben-Amos, *The Culture of Giving*, op. cit., p.338.
8. William Salt Library M762.
9. British Library A.i.1 – C.viii.3.
10. Worth, R.N. *Calendar of the Tavistock Parish Records.* 1887, pp.57–63.
11. Index to Parish Returns towards the rebuilding of St Paul's Cathedral, c.1678: www.history.ac.uk/gh/briefs.htm. The documents have recently been moved to London Metropolitan Archives and no doubt this page will soon appear on its website.
12. Povah, Alfred, ed. *The Annals of the Parishes of St Olave, Hart Street and All Hallows, Staining.* (Blades, East & Blades, 1894), p.222.

13. Herbert, George. *A Priest to the Temple.* (Thomas Whittaker, 1908), p.80.

Chapter Ten: Other Miscellaneous Records

1. Burgess, Clive, ed. *The Pre-Reformation Records of All Saints', Bristol: Wills, the Halleway Chantry Records and Deeds.* (Bristol Record Society 56, 2004).
2. The questions posed in one such book of articles are outlined in Peyton, Sidney A., ed. *The Churchwardens' Presentments in the Oxfordshire Peculiars of Dorchester, Thame and Banbury.* (Oxfordshire Record Society 10, 1928), pp.xiii–xv.
3. Craig, J.S. 'Co-operation and Initiatives: Churchwardens and the Parish Accounts of Mildenhall', *Social History* 18(3), 1993, p.362.
4. Arnold, F.H. 'Sussex Certificates for the Royal Touch', *Sussex Archaeological Collections* 25, 1873, p.210.

SUBJECT INDEX

PERSONAL INDEX

PLACE NAME INDEX